NEGOTIATE
IT
RIGHT

NEGOTIATE
IT
RIGHT

16 RULES FOR LANDING
THE BEST JOB OFFER

KAMAL GUPTA

JAICO PUBLISHING HOUSE

Ahmedabad Bangalore Chennai
Delhi Hyderabad Kolkata Mumbai

DISCLAIMER

The information contained in this book is provided for general informational purposes only and should not be taken as legal, financial, or professional advice. The author and publisher disclaim any liability arising directly or indirectly from the use of this material. Readers should consult with qualified professionals before making decisions based on the content herein.

Published by Jaico Publishing House
A-2 Jash Chambers, 7-A Sir Phirozshah Mehta Road
Fort, Mumbai - 400 001
jaicopub@jaicobooks.com
www.jaicobooks.com

To be sold only in India, Bangladesh, Bhutan, Pakistan, Nepal, Sri Lanka and the Maldives.

NEGOTIATE IT RIGHT
ISBN 978-93-49358-36-2

First Jaico Impression: 2025

Printed by
Trinity Academy For Corporate Training Limited, Mumbai

CONTENTS

INTRODUCTION

You don't get what you deserve; you get what you negotiate.

I STRONGLY BELIEVE that negotiating is one of life's more important skills. The world is often an unfair place, and many people will seek to take advantage of you. The best way I know to counter this is by out-negotiating them. When you do so, you will find that even a short time spent negotiating can be extremely profitable, perhaps more than any other activity. You don't need to be a professional to negotiate effectively; it is a skill anyone can develop with practice. My goal in this book is to provide a few simple rules to help you get started.

The most important fact to realize is that every negotiation has a single objective: to convince the other side to give up their position and adopt yours. This seemingly straightforward task is complicated by the fact that your opponent has the exact same goal—only in reverse. These conflicting objectives turn any negotiation into a battle of wits, with each party striving to outmaneuver the other. If you magically find yourself in a negotiation that stays conflict-free from start to finish, look carefully. The odds are that you are about to get ripped off. As with any game of skill, winning or losing in negotiation is a function of a player's ability and experience.

Without a doubt, the most meaningful negotiation in our lives is for our jobs. Your salary today will have a profound effect on your tomorrow, significantly impacting where you live, the quality of education your children receive, your access to healthcare, and much more. As a result, all other negotiations pale in comparison to what we can manage to get paid for our work.

It is also increasingly likely that your next job-related negotiation will be with a large company[1], as just 0.3 percent of businesses in the United States employ more than half of the private-sector workforce. A quarter-century of consolidation has led to every major industry in the United States—including airlines, media, and finance—being dominated by a handful of corporations. Continuous mergers and acquisitions have reduced the number of publicly listed companies in the United States by nearly half, from 8,090 in 1996 to approximately 4,000 in 2024[2]. The resulting lack of competition has tilted the playing field further in favor of big business and against workers.

To make matters worse, a dangerous new ethos took hold in the United States during the 1990s: CEOs became accountable only to their shareholders. This mindset absolved the titans of industry of any responsibility toward their employees, customers,

---

[1] Defined as having 500 or more employees

[2] In contrast, the number of publicly listed companies worldwide has risen from nearly 31,000 in 1996 to around 55,000 today.

or the country itself. Profit became the be-all and end-all of a corporation's existence and its share price the only metric of success. In their hunt for ever-larger profits, corporations have used their political and financial might to run roughshod over the American populace and torn the very fabric of society. Whether it is the sharp rise in inequality, the intense political polarization, or the opioid crisis, many of the significant problems plaguing the country today are the result of corporate greed running wild.

These problems are by no means exclusive to America, as growing corporate power has become a global phenomenon. It has reshaped economies, influenced the democratic process, and exacerbated inequalities across continents. Take India, for instance, where the increasing power of big conglomerates has led to even greater inequality. In 2024, the top 1% of households in the United States owned 30.8% of the country's wealth, whereas in India, this figure was 40.1%. As the gap between the rich and the poor widens, it fuels growing resentment among the masses toward the "elite." The rise of far-right populism in Western democracies is partly a result of the increasing economic insecurity felt by low-skilled workers. These voters feel abandoned by mainstream politics, making them susceptible to the anti-establishment rhetoric of these parties. The rapid growth of transnational corporations has also worsened the effects of climate change as goods criss-cross the globe, burning more and more fuel.

When I arrived in the United States as a young immigrant in the 1980s, I was struck by the fact that anyone willing to work could get a job and attain a decent standard of living. Thanks to three decades of corporatism, that is no longer the case. A rise in corporate power contributed to the inflation-adjusted median household income remaining stagnant for a quarter of a century (from $62,260 in 1989 to $64,900 in 2014[3]), even as the real GDP doubled and the stock market surged nearly six-fold. Virtually all of the economic gains of this 25-year period went to capital at the expense of labor. It is one thing, however, to move a factory overseas to save on labor costs, but it is entirely another to leave newly unemployed workers stranded without any support or alternative employment opportunities. The former, it can be argued, makes economic sense, but the latter is undeniably heartless. This story has been repeated countless times across the United States and has contributed to the hollowing out of the industrial heartland.

Despite the situation appearing bleak, there is still hope. Corporations need people, or rather, employees, to achieve their one and only objective, which is to generate higher profits. Consequently, the greater the profit potential a company sees in an individual, the more it is willing to negotiate with them. Nothing illustrates this phenomenon more clearly than Wall Street, where I have worked for the past three decades. While I learned to negotiate at an early age, it was the financial industry that helped me to fine-tune my skills.

I have used that expertise to benefit not only myself but many others as well. Since 1999, I have helped countless people negotiate employment contracts with a variety of financial institutions, including investment banks, hedge funds, money managers, and insurance companies. Despite the immense power

---

[3] In 2022 dollars, according to the Federal Reserve Bank of St. Louis

wielded by these behemoths, I have consistently managed to help individuals overcome their corporate adversaries. I have done this for decades, yet no company has ever learned of my involvement. I have always operated strictly behind the scenes, like a shadow negotiator.

Readers familiar with my 2022 memoir, *Play It Right*, will know that I have a long history of combating unfairness wherever I encounter it. As the book recounts, while still in my twenties, I gave up on a promising career in computers to become a professional blackjack player. I was fascinated by the game of twenty-one, but even more so, I was outraged by the fact that casinos barred card-counters. This meant the gambling houses of Nevada were only willing to cater to those who could be easily parted from their money. Any gambler who had the audacity to use their brain while playing blackjack was summarily ejected from the premises—a fate I suffered on multiple occasions. As a result, I was forced to engage in a variety of deceptions just so I could continue to play. Blackjack became a form of guerilla warfare for me, much like negotiating is today.

It is worth pointing out that I purposefully avoided playing poker in casinos for one simple reason—the house always wins. Casinos take a cut from every pot, which makes it impossible for them to lose money. Consequently, gamblers sitting around a poker table are battling each other, not the establishment. A blackjack player, on the other hand, goes up against the house, which was my primary motivation for playing the game. I had no desire to defeat (or be defeated by) other individuals like me, as is required in poker. At the same time, I am fascinated by the intellectual challenge posed by the game, especially because of its similarities to negotiating.

Poker and negotiating are both games of incomplete information, where players try to intuit their opponents' position from their actions. Furthermore, both games require a high degree of skill, with the superior player usually emerging victorious. It should come as no surprise, then, that many of the strategies described in this book are inspired by poker.

In an extraordinary turn of events, my gambling skills brought me to Wall Street, the last place I ever expected to be. As *Play It Right* describes in gory detail, I was repelled by the abusive practices of investment banks and spent decades combating them. Even my investment strategy for beating financial markets turned into a fight against unfairness, this time targeting the pricing of various securities. I would start by determining the fair value of a trade construct and then sell financial instruments that were priced unfairly high and buy those that were priced unfairly low. Furthermore, as was the case with blackjack, the time I spent managing money was also akin to David fighting Goliath. In a market dominated by large money managers and banks, my trade sizes were small and barely registered on their radar. Despite the substantial size disadvantage, I managed to repeatedly outmaneuver these giants and compiled what is quite possibly the finest long-term track record of managing money in hedge fund history.

It is also worth emphasizing that, despite having spent most of my life in casinos and on Wall Street, I have never been motivated by money. This is not an accident. Money, for me, has always been the side effect of a game played well; it is not the primary objective. As long as I play the game correctly, I am confident that money will follow. This principle has stood me in good stead in casinos, on Wall Street, and during every negotiation.

I strictly adhered to my card-counting system for the entire time I played blackjack. Despite suffering innumerable losing streaks, I insisted on playing every hand according to the odds, never relying on gut instinct. Likewise, in two decades of managing money, I never once deviated from my investment methodology. Not even the great financial crisis of 2008 could dislodge me from my chosen strategy. It is no different in negotiating, where I have consistently focused on the process and not the end result. With hundreds of deals under my belt, I can confidently state that success was the result of focusing on the game, and not on money.

My years of negotiating have taught me many valuable lessons, which I have condensed into 16 rules. Each of these rules is presented in a separate chapter in this book, along with examples from real-life cases in which I was personally involved. These rules are not specific to any industry or country, as corporations are the same everywhere when it comes to prioritizing profits over people. These rules are not dependent on the amounts involved either; they apply equally whether you are negotiating for $5,000 or $5 million.

In terms of money alone, negotiating yields a remarkably high return on the time invested. As a graduate student, I once spent 30 minutes negotiating $100 off a used car. That run-rate—$200 per hour—was an order of magnitude higher than my salary upon graduation. Two decades later, during my Wall Street years, I routinely managed to extract six- and seven-figure sums from large corporations while spending no more than 10–20 hours on any individual situation.

There are some who find bargaining distasteful and consider it beneath their dignity. As far as I am concerned, these folks either have too much money or too little appreciation for the game. I find negotiating to be a great sport and a good cause. Few things give me greater satisfaction than securing a good deal for a client—I refer to whoever I negotiate for as a client, though I have never collected any payment for my services. My reward is knowing that I have played the game well and possibly injected a small measure of fairness into the world. It is for this reason that I help only individuals to negotiate against corporations, and never the other way around.

I negotiate for others because I can, and because I know the power of a good deal. A well-executed negotiation not only improves your financial health but also lifts your spirits. Likewise, the scars of a poor outcome can persist for years, if not decades. During my long tenure, I have witnessed both phenomena on numerous occasions.

Becoming a competent negotiator requires practice. My rules are designed to help you get started on that journey. I have listed them in their order of importance, with the more critical ones appearing first. However, it is possible that some of the later ones are more relevant to your specific situation. I would urge you to glance at every chapter and then focus on the ones that are most applicable to your current circumstances. Hopefully, this book will help you achieve your desired objectives.

CHAPTER 1

FOCUS ON THE NEXT MOVE, AND *ONLY* THE NEXT MOVE

EXPERIENCE HAS TAUGHT me that the key to a successful outcome in a negotiation is a single-minded focus on the next move, and *only* the next move. Looking any further ahead is a waste of time and effort, and it may even prove detrimental to your cause. Therefore, the winning strategy for a negotiation is the opposite of that for chess, where players must think several moves ahead.

Negotiating and chess are both games of skill where the better player usually wins. But that is where the similarity ends. Chess is a finite game with well-defined rules for how each piece can move across the board—for instance, a bishop must move diagonally and a rook only horizontally or vertically. Consequently, while you cannot know what the other player is thinking or the strategy they plan to follow, there is never any mystery as to what they *can* do. That is not to say that chess is easy, only that it is finite.

Negotiating, on the other hand, is an infinite game with limitless possibilities. It is not confined to an eight-by-eight board or a fixed set of pieces that can only be moved in a preset manner. A negotiator is free to invent new pieces and move them in ways that confound the opponent. To try and predict the course of a negotiation is an exercise in futility. So, I don't even try. Instead, when it is my turn to act, I examine all of the available information and formulate the best possible response to the situation. Once that reply has been delivered, I stop thinking about the matter. I begin contemplating my next move only after the other side has made theirs or if new information comes to light. This back-and-forth continues either until an agreement is reached or the playing field is abandoned. It is important to note that not every negotiation results in a deal; sometimes, the two sides are simply too far apart. While this may seem like an undesirable outcome, the information gained during the encounter can, at times, be more valuable than a signed contract. This is what happened in one of my cases where the first two candidates (both my clients) turned down an investment bank's offer. By the time the same job was offered to a third individual—also my advisee—I knew that the bank was desperate. That information, combined with the knowledge of the amounts that had been offered to the first two candidates, allowed me to extract a substantially larger sum for the third.

NOT "WHAT IF?" BUT "WHAT NOW?"

There is no place in a negotiation for the question "what if?". However, virtually everyone that I've ever negotiated for ends up posing it. Whenever that occurs, I explain to the individual that the only question that matters during a negotiation is "what now?". My refusal to speculate about the future is usually met with confusion and bewilderment. That feeling, however, is temporary and disappears by the time we reach the end of the negotiation. And when I negotiate for them the next time around—the vast majority of my clients are repeat customers—they stop questioning my methods.

During any negotiation, I try to impose a sense of order on what is essentially a chaotic process. Even the simplest of deals follows an unpredictable path while complicated ones can feel like a wild roller-coaster ride, rife with twists and turns. Unlike a roller coaster, however, a negotiation does not deliver the same thrills on each ride. The hundreds of situations that I have been involved in have all followed their own erratic paths. This sounds like a cliché, but the only predictable thing about a negotiation is its unpredictability. Sometimes, the process is over in a week, and at other times, you are scrambling for a resolution several months later. I have even conducted negotiations that spanned three calendar years. The longer the process, the greater the uncertainty. Managers might quit or get fired. Companies may suddenly impose a hiring freeze, or worse, go bankrupt. There is also the chance that your prospective boss changes their mind or a better candidate comes along. There is no limit to the range of possible events that can upend even the best-laid plans.

WHY NEGOTIATIONS ARE UNPREDICTABLE

The individual you are most likely to encounter in your dealings with a corporation is a mid-level manager. Contrary to what one might expect, this manager does not wield a great deal of authority inside the organization. Their role is more akin to that of a salesman at a car dealership who needs to get approval from the boss at every step of the negotiation.

The real power in a corporation is wielded by unseen forces: senior executives, human resources (HR) representatives, and lawyers. The senior managers decide what everyone gets paid, HR ensures that the company is protected at all times, and the lawyers' job is to come up with creative ways to stiff the employees contractually. It is this machinery that has the final say about an individual's fate, not the person fronting for them. This is why negotiations with a corporation are inherently unpredictable. You are never just dealing with someone that you've encountered face-to-face, but with an edifice that remains hidden. If I had a penny for every time I've heard a manager say, "It was out of my hands," I would have a lot of pennies.

Given that a corporation's decision-making process remains inscrutable to most, it stands to reason that its actions are inherently impossible to predict. Consequently, the most important quality in a negotiator is not the capacity to forecast the future, but the ability to adapt to unexpected situations. I have yet to be involved in a negotiation that proceeded according to plan, without any surprises. Therefore, even after a quarter-century of negotiating, I approach every new encounter with an open mind and without any preconceived notions about what the other side might do. That approach allows me to respond to every situation on its own merits, especially when corporations attempt to pull a fast one—an all-too-frequent occurrence.

BE MINDFUL OF THE BAIT AND SWITCH

One of the more frustrating things about negotiating with large companies is their propensity to indulge in a bait and switch. As we shall see throughout the book, corporations frequently say one thing and then draft paperwork that says something entirely different. Adding insult to injury, every contract explicitly states that "This agreement supersedes any verbal agreement between the two parties." I have encountered this phenomenon nearly every time that I have negotiated for myself.

Early in my career, I found myself staring at a hedge fund contract that was filled with clauses that bore no resemblance to the agreement that I had reached with the firm's owners. I spent an exasperating hour with the document before confronting the firm's general counsel (GC).

"Are you willfully trying to screw me?" I asked him bluntly.

The lawyer's reply left me stunned.

"Yes, Kamal. That's what we do with every employee. Don't tell me that you're surprised."

The GC's reply made it clear that the game was rigged, and not in my favor. The game was what it was, and nothing I could do or say was going to change it. However, the choice—to play or not to play—was mine. I chose to play, and not just for myself.

I started with the GC himself. With the help of my attorney, I took a scalpel to his contract, slicing it every which way. A few weeks later, we had managed to excise all of the problematic clauses as well as insert new ones that were in my favor. The owners conceded because my performance over the past two years had been flawless. The final version of the contract turned out to be so advantageous for me that just six months later, the company wanted to renegotiate.

"Why?" I asked the GC.

"Things have changed," he replied.

"Things always change," I said. "That's why we have contracts."

"Why don't you at least listen to what we are proposing?" the lawyer pleaded.

I didn't need to. A renegotiation, by definition, is designed to leave you worse off than before. Otherwise, why would the company bother? I could have simply refused to renegotiate, but I decided to ask the lawyer a leading question instead.

"What if we can't agree on a new contract?"

"In that case, we'll have to buy you out of your old one," he replied.

I knew right then that's what I wanted. I spent the next two weeks pretending to negotiate with the company before throwing my hands up and saying, "We are not getting anywhere. I think you should just buy me out."

The hedge fund's owners had also grown frustrated with me, which had been my intent all along. They agreed to the terms of my buyout, and I left the company with two extra years' worth of compensation in my pocket—the remaining term of my original contract. As I made my way out the door, I could only marvel at the distance between where the firm had started and where we ended up. This experience has served as a blueprint for many of my future dealings where, far more often than not, I have managed to turn the tables on Goliath.

RESIST THE URGE TO GIVE A KNEE-JERK RESPONSE

Whenever your opponent makes an unexpected move—a fairly regular occurrence in my experience—resist the urge to give them a quick response. A knee-jerk reaction on your part, no matter whether positive or negative, is more likely to hurt your cause than to help it. Instead, it is best to slow the process down and deliver a simple reply, "Let me think about it. I'll call you back." This allows you to temporarily retreat from the battlefield and plot your next move while also making it possible to seek advice, as is the case with most of my clients.

Another example of a corporation pulling a stunt occurred when I was helping an unemployed bond trader negotiate with an investment bank. The hard-fought battle lasted for a month, but we managed to secure an excellent deal. Or so I thought. Thomas (not his real name) was thrilled, but it was too early for me to celebrate. Verbal agreements are meaningless by themselves, and I had seen plenty of negotiations fall apart at this stage.

That's what happened here as well. The problem began with a phone call from Thomas's future boss.

"We will have the contract ready by tomorrow," he said.

"Great!" Thomas replied.

The manager's next utterance came out of left field.

"Just wanted to let you know that the amount we'd discussed will be prorated for the eight months left in the year."

"Wait! What?" Thomas exclaimed.

"It is April now. You will only be working here for part of the year, so we will prorate the amount accordingly."

Thomas was dumbfounded, but, wisely, did not react any further. Instead, he delivered the standard reply.

"Let me think about it. I'll call you back."

I was furious when I heard what the investment bank had done. In one fell swoop, the company had lowered my client's pay by one-third. In two decades of negotiating Wall Street contracts, I had seen plenty of bait and switches but never one like this. In every single case, the amount discussed was the amount written into the contract, whether there were ten months left in the year or just two. That's why big-ticket contracts are usually handed out at the beginning of the year and almost never toward the end. Also, this job opening was the result of a trader (coincidentally, another client of mine) leaving the bank for a competitor. He had left four months' worth of earnings behind that rightfully belonged to his replacement. Those are Wall Street's rules, and every investment bank abides by them. These managers had either just dreamed up this new wrinkle, or they were simply trying to take advantage of my client. Regardless, they couldn't be allowed to get away with it.

DON'T BE AFRAID TO PUSH BACK

No one is ever going to hand you a good deal; you will have to fight for it. In almost every negotiation, there comes a point when you will have to push back against the company. For Thomas, that moment was now.

"Tell them that you are out," I said, much to his shock.

"Are you serious?"

"Yes. Also say that you refuse to work at a company that negotiates in such bad faith."

"I understand, but this is still a high number. If push comes to shove, I would take it."

"You can't! If you let them get away with this, who knows what else they will pull once you start working there?"

"So, what do you want me to say?" he asked, his voice filled with a sense of despair.

"Tell the manager that prorating contracts is not the industry standard and that this is making you wonder if you even want to work there. So, if they insist upon dropping your pay by a third, then you are no longer interested in the position."

"Are you sure? It seems very aggressive."

"There is no other alternative. They are trying to pull the wool over your eyes, and this is the only way to make them behave. If they want this process to get back on track, then the boss's boss needs to call you and apologize."

"The boss's boss? He'll never do that." Thomas was incredulous.

"We'll see."

I hadn't recommended this course of action out of bravado. Despite the fact that Thomas's negotiating position was weak—he was currently unemployed—I felt that we had the upper hand. Everyone who had interviewed him had reiterated that he was exactly what they were looking for. Moreover, a Wall Street trading desk often has hundreds of millions of dollars at stake. How could they afford to walk away from their perfect candidate over a few hundred thousand dollars? Sometimes, it is less about the cards you hold and more about how you play them.

Nor was I acting out of a sense of righteousness—there's no place for that in a negotiation. The driving imperative for me, as always, was a practical one: How do I secure the best possible deal for my client?

It takes a great deal of courage to turn down a seven-figure contract, especially when you haven't worked in years. But Thomas managed to do it. He called the hiring manager and told him to take a hike, albeit a little more politely than I would have done. As I had expected, it induced a small panic in his future boss. The only thing he could muster was an incoherent, "Let me see what we can do," before Thomas hung up.

Having done as I had asked, Thomas went to bed that night feeling miserable. I, on the other hand, was convinced that we had made the right move and would deal with the chips as they fell. I was also confident that in the unlikely event of the negotiation falling apart, I would find a way to resuscitate it afterwards. For now, though, the ball was in the company's court, and I was back to waiting for it to return.

It came back the next morning in the form of a call from the boss's boss. To Thomas's great surprise, he apologized profusely.

"I understand why you are upset. We should have made this clear from the very beginning. How do we bring this matter back on track?"

This time my client didn't need to confer with me before responding. We knew exactly what we wanted.

"Why don't we go back to the amount that we'd discussed?"

"We can't do that," the boss's boss implored.

"In that case, what can you do?" a freshly empowered Thomas asked.

"The most we can do is 80 percent of the original number."

To say that Thomas was thrilled would be an understatement.

If it were up to him, he would have accepted on the spot. Nevertheless, he maintained his cool and delivered the scripted reply.

"Let me think about it. I'll call you back."

The senior manager tried hard to get Thomas to say yes over the phone, but Thomas held firm. It was clear to both parties that the company had lost control and that the individual was now in the driver's seat.

I too was happy to hear of the new and improved number. But even more than that, I was glad that our move had been the right one.

"What do you want to do, Thomas?"

"I really want to accept, but you tell me."

KNOW WHEN TO STOP PUSHING

As important as it is to know when to push your adversary, it is equally vital to know when to stop pushing. The goal in a negotiation is not to destroy your opponent but to get the best possible deal out of them. In this case, even though the amount was lower than what I would have liked, I felt that we had pushed the investment bank far enough. Given Thomas's aggressive stance the night before, the boss's boss knew that he had just one shot at bringing him back to the negotiating table. Hence, I was convinced that he had led with the best possible offer. Pressing him any further ran the risk of jeopardizing the deal.

I asked Thomas to let the big guy sweat for two hours before accepting his terms. A quicker acceptance might have made him wonder if he had paid too much (which I believe he had).

"Ha ha! Okay," my client said, now in a considerably better mood.

A few days later, after the dust had settled and the contracts had been signed, Thomas admitted that he would have botched the whole thing if he had followed his own instincts.

WHEN A CLIENT INSISTS ON SPECULATING ABOUT THE FUTURE

Unfortunately, not every client is as amenable as Thomas. Despite my best efforts to the contrary, some insist on not only posing the "what-if" question but also answering it themselves. One of those clients—I'll call him Fred—boldly predicted how the game would unfold as soon as the first move had been made. Right after the company had called him, even before a single interview had been conducted, he claimed that he would get hired and for how much.

"Seriously?" I asked.

"Yes. I know the market, and I know these guys."

I knew the market as well and was convinced that he was too high. As far as knowing "these guys" was concerned, that was an impossibility. I tried to rein him in but to no avail. He strutted through the interviews only to have the company turn him down. The rejection stunned Fred, and in return, he trained his sights on the management.

"Those bastards!" he exclaimed, paying no attention to my attempts to explain where he had gone wrong. This is a prime example of an individual's preconceived ideas getting in their way. He would have been much better off walking into the situation with an open mind instead of acting as if the job was already his.

One might wonder why I take on clients who are not willing to listen. I believe that no matter how difficult the individual, I can still be of some assistance to them. At the very least, I can help them prepare for their interviews, and if they are successful, I can help them vet the contract. More importantly, though, I welcome every opportunity to improve my craft. I love this game, and there are only so many times I can play it for myself. Besides, every negotiation allows me to gain valuable information about the state of the job market and the culture of a company. That information proves immensely valuable in my future dealings, sometimes even against the same opponent. As we shall see in a later chapter, information represents power in a negotiation.

IN CONCLUSION

The key to success in negotiating lies in adapting to events as they unfold, not in being able to predict them beforehand. As in life, you have little control over what might happen during a negotiation. It is, however, completely within your control how you react to those events, unpredictable though they might be. As long as you make every small move carefully and rationally, the big picture will take care of itself. Just remember, the only question that matters in a negotiation is "what now?".

CHAPTER 2

NEVER GIVE OUT THE FIRST NUMBER

"WHAT WOULD IT take for us to hire you?" is the most seductive question that you'll face during an interview. It also happens to be the most dangerous and one that you must not answer. This cardinal rule is one that I insist every client abides by, no ifs, ands, or buts. The corporation *has* to come up with a number first.

In the history of negotiating, no one has ever ended up getting more than what they asked for. As a result, your answer to this question immediately places an upper bound on your compensation. Moreover, it is nearly impossible to get the amount right. You will end up quoting either too high or too low, both of which suffer from major drawbacks. The former makes you appear greedy, and the latter runs the risk of being quickly accepted. Therefore, it is of utmost importance that the other side go first.

Managers will try hard to get a number out of you. Given that an outright refusal to answer a question is seldom advisable during an interview, you're left with no option but to deflect when faced with, "What would it take?" It is for these situations that I ask every client to memorize a short script and deliver it as their reply to the offending question.

"I haven't thought about money. I came here to see if there's a fit. If I'm the right person for you and this is the right company for me, then I'm sure money won't be a problem."

Money is always a problem, and everyone knows it. Despite that, no company has ever pushed back against this little speech of mine. It would be unseemly for managers to insist upon discussing money when the candidate is aspiring for a nobler purpose. Consequently, this short answer works just as well for a junior position as it does for a senior role.

A GAME OF IMPERFECT INFORMATION

In any negotiation, neither side can see the whole picture. Only you know the cards that you hold and the terms you are willing to accept. However, you don't have any idea about your opponent's cards or about the concessions that they are willing to make. This makes negotiating similar to poker, another game where part of the information remains hidden. A negotiator, much like a poker player, attempts to deduce the opponent's hand by deciphering their moves. As with any game of imperfect information, the key to a successful outcome is your position on the table.

In the most popular of poker games, Texas Hold'em, the player who acts first is said to be *under the gun* because they are forced to act without any knowledge about the rest of the table's cards. Conversely, the player that goes last can make the most informed decision by virtue of having observed the actions of all the other players. It is for this reason that a medium-strength hand, such as a pair of sevens, gets folded in an early position but invites a raise from a later position, especially when most players have folded beforehand.

The strategy in playing poker is to try and draw an error from your opponent(s). The goal is to get them to either fold a hand that is superior to yours or to call with one that is inferior. I find this to be the most fascinating aspect of poker: *The best hand does not always win.* The same is true for how I negotiate. I try to provoke the corporation into making a mistake and paying more than it should, something that occurs far more regularly than people realize.

MAKE SURE THE COMPANY OFFERS YOU THE JOB FIRST

A corporation's opening number is meaningless unless it is accompanied with the words "We'd like to hire you." This simple statement commits the managers to a decision, and negotiations can move forward. Although the offer is only verbal at this stage, and not legally binding, it is still an important step in the process. In a quarter-century of negotiating, I have yet to come across a company that has lied about their intention to hire a candidate. Therefore, I insist that every client make sure that they are being offered the job before discussing numbers. Until that occurs, I ask the individual to stick with, "We can talk about money when you have settled upon me as your chosen candidate."

Once you have managed to get a number out of the company, the first thing to consider is whether it is at the market level. I have a firm rule about acting last in a negotiation, but that does not mean that I am unaware of the going rate for the position in question. A combination of past dealings and a few strategically placed phone calls (usually to former clients) allows me to discover this information relatively quickly. I would recommend that you too get the lay of the land before entering into a serious negotiation.

DEFLECT AS MUCH AS NECESSARY

As mentioned earlier, you must do whatever you can to avoid answering the question, "What would it take?" Not only is it the right play strategically, but it can also lead to you being pleasantly surprised by the company's opening offer. That's what happened to a friend (and also a client) of mine after days of artful deflection on her part.

A multi-billion dollar pharmaceutical company had searched high and low for their first-ever head of administration before settling on my friend. That's when the infamous question reared its ugly head.

"What would it take for you to come here?"

As instructed, she refused to answer, reverting instead to my standard reply of seeking the right fit. The CEO, in response, tried a different tack.

"We've never hired a head of administration before. We have no idea about the appropriate compensation for the position. Can you help us out and let us know what you would accept?"

This was disingenuous on many levels. First, even if the CEO had "no idea" about the appropriate pay for the job, all he had to do was to pick up the phone and call a few headhunters.

More importantly, no company advertises for an open position without knowing beforehand what it is willing to pay. It is this piece of information that I was after.

"I understand that this is your first time filling this role. Still, you must have budgeted an amount for the position. Why don't we start from there?" she replied.

"We haven't."

I was convinced that this wasn't true, but calling your opponent a liar to their face is never a good idea. So, she continued to deflect.

"I see. But you must know where this individual fits in your organization. Perhaps the compensation of other employees at the same level would provide a clue."

The CEO tried hard, but my client would not relent. Her resolve was likely due to the fact that this was my fifth time helping her negotiate. Together, we had overcome many adversaries over the past decade, including several that were far more challenging than this one. The CEO, having failed in numerous attempts to get any sort of number out of her, caved in.

"We can offer you a salary of $500,000," he said, causing her jaw to drop.

At the time, I had no idea why the company had started so high, nor did I care. The important thing was that the CEO had overshot the mark, and not by a small margin. My friend and I had discussed compensation at length—something I do with every client—and we had agreed that a salary in the vicinity of $250,000 was fair. Had she been *under the gun*, she would not have dared to ask for more than $300,000. Instead, by sticking to her guns, she had managed to extract an astonishing offer from the company.

"Let me think about it. I'll call you back," she replied, as always.

WHEN THE NUMBER IS HIGH, ACCEPT GRACEFULLY

I was thrilled with the company's offer. I briefly contemplated trying for an even higher amount but decided against it. Protocol dictates that once you quote a counteroffer, you can no longer count on the original offer still being on the table. This is what makes negotiating so fraught: *There is no risk-free move.* Every step you take has the effect of potentially erasing what was on the table before. Had we countered the CEO with, say, $550,000, there was a chance of losing the $500,000. Also, time works against you when there is an excellent offer on the table. The best move is to accept it as gracefully as possible, which is precisely what she did, after waiting for a couple of hours.

It would take us a few months to figure out that the pharmaceutical company had, in fact, not overpaid my friend after all, at least not by their standards. Over time, she discovered that the company had an overly generous pay policy for all of its senior employees and for many members of the rank and file. This critical piece of information was not available to us during the negotiation. Nevertheless, by refusing to name her price, she had ensured that she would not be underpaid versus the rest of the firm. While a disparity of this magnitude (between expectation and reality) is rare, it is still of vital importance that you do not quote the opening number. Then, and only then, is there a chance that your expectations might be exceeded.

WHEN THE NUMBER IS LOW, GIVE NO INFORMATION

Unfortunately, not every company starts high. It is far more common for employers to go low on the opening number. Whenever that occurs, I refuse to give any counteroffer. By making a lowball offer, the company has risked nothing. So, it deserves nothing in return. Anything other than a simple "That won't work" would give the company free information.

An example of a company going low involved a Long Island hospital chain attempting to recruit a cancer specialist. Without displaying an iota of shame, the hospital executives offered my client 20 percent *less* than his current salary. Rightfully, they should have offered him at least 20 percent more, especially because relocating to suburban New York City would have significantly increased his cost of living.

"Sorry, I don't think that will work," the doctor replied.

"In that case, what will work?" Same question, different words.

"I think we are too far apart for that," is my standard recommended reply in these situations.

The company knew exactly what my client was getting paid at the time, and they had to have known that 80 cents on the dollar wasn't going to cut it. So, why had they done it? Perhaps this was just a pricing exercise for them to figure out what to pay *other* doctors, or maybe even to another candidate. As with the pharmaceutical company, the hospital chain also tried hard to get a number out of my client, but to no avail. The company's offer was meaningless—they knew full well that it would never be accepted—so we refused to negotiate. They badgered my client for days before giving up. Interestingly, throughout that time, the hospital executives staunchly refused to go any higher, thereby confirming my suspicions that they were not serious about hiring my client.

MAINTAIN YOUR COOL WHILE REJECTING AN OFFER

Not every employer is willing to admit defeat this readily. It is not unusual for bosses to become downright unpleasant upon suffering a rejection (the refusal to give a counteroffer is tantamount to turning the company down). In these situations, I ask the individual to stay calm and remember that they are the one in charge. That is not to say that there is no room for anger in a negotiation, but that is a topic for a later chapter.

A West Coast money manager displayed particularly poor form while attempting to recruit a research analyst. The firm's HR representative tried repeatedly to get a number out of my client but failed. As is usually the case, this company also capitulated and came up with a starting offer.

"What do you think of $275,000?" said the lady from HR.

"Are you offering me the job?" my client asked, as instructed.

The HR representative was taken aback by the question. She pondered for a short while before replying, "Yes, we'd like to hire you."

The investment company's number was far too low. At the time, my client was getting paid almost a third higher, and that too at a far more prestigious institution. The company was either unaware of her market value or simply trying to steal her away. Regardless, our answer was fairly straightforward.

"I am sorry, but that won't work," my client replied.

"In that case, what will work?"

"We are too far apart for that."

The lady from HR hung up the phone in frustration, only to return two hours later.

"I am very sorry, but I made a mistake. I was looking at the wrong pay scales. We can go up to $325,000."

I didn't believe this for a second. HR representatives are the voice of the company, especially when it comes to hiring and firing individuals. They are trained to speak with great care to any current or future employee. Under no circumstances would they make job offers after erroneously looking at the "wrong pay scales." It was more likely that she had relayed my client's refusal to the hiring managers, who, in turn, had decided to raise the offer by $50,000. The HR representative could have said as much, but she was perhaps trying to shield the managers by taking all the blame upon herself.

By now, my client and I had given up hope of reaching a satisfactory conclusion to this negotiation. The gap between the two sides was too large, and the company's improvement was too small. So, she turned them down once again.

"Thank you very much for the offer, but I am unable to accept."

"Would a different number work?"

"I'm not sure," she replied, being evasive on purpose.

In normal circumstances, that should have been enough to close the matter. But not in this case. Once again, the HR representative passed on my client's response to the hiring manager, who was not pleased. He decided to cut out the intermediary and call my client himself.

"This is not how you are supposed to negotiate," he shouted, his anger palpable over the phone.

I had to laugh when I heard this. Since when does a player take advice from their opponent? Moreover, contrary to what the manager had claimed, this is exactly how you are supposed to negotiate. If you are not serious about working for a company, then you cannot give them any number whatsoever. What if they agreed to your terms? In that case, it would be in poor taste for you to still turn them down. You might think that quoting an absurdly high number would protect you, but more likely than not, it would infuriate the managers and potentially invite retaliation. The best option in these situations is to refuse to name your price, no matter how great the pressure. The worst that can happen is that the company will get annoyed and drop the negotiations.

My client managed to retain her composure despite a sustained onslaught from the manager. She turned the job down for a third time, thereby ensuring that this crew would never hire her in the future. Burning a few bridges, however, is an unavoidable part of any war.

I have also come across managers who, when faced with a rejection, tried to claim that they were offering the individual a partnership, and not merely an employer-employee relationship. This too is laughable because there is no such thing (other than a legally documented partnership, of course). Corporations would cease to function if bosses suddenly started treating employees as equals.

WHEN THE NUMBER IS IN THE RIGHT BALLPARK, TREAD CAREFULLY

The response to a company's opening offer being too high or too low is fairly straightforward: accept gracefully or refuse to engage, respectively. However, it is a far more delicate situation when the company's starting number (or their second or third attempt) happens to be in the right area. I define the "right area" as any amount that is consistent with the market price for the position. At this point, I shift gears and try to gently guide the future bosses toward an even higher amount. The probability of a successful outcome has increased dramatically, and it is a good idea to maintain (or, if needed, restore) goodwill. I may ask for a slightly higher salary, additional stock options, or a sign-on bonus. The goal at this stage is to look for small increments while making sure that the latest offer stays intact. Consequently, I take the opposite line.

"I think your offer is reasonable, and I'm inclined to accept. However, my decision would be a lot easier if you could just…"

You will be surprised how often this simple line yields results. It gives the company hope that the candidate will soon be theirs, which provides them with an incentive to sweeten the pot a little more—corporations prefer their worker bees to be enthusiastic. By saying "I'm inclined to accept," you ensure that the offer won't get pulled simply because you asked for a little more. I have never observed a negotiation fall apart at this stage, so it's worth a try. Remember, any incremental concession that you can wrangle from the company will persist for as long as you work there, and likely for the rest of your career.

THE DOWNSIDE OF YOUR QUOTING THE FIRST NUMBER

As mentioned earlier, your answer to the question, "What would it take?" instantly places an upper bound on your pay. However, there is another important reason why you should never answer that question: It is impossible to get the answer right because there are too many variables. Even if an individual knows the market price for their skills, they cannot possibly know about the internal workings of the corporation. Whether the company is desperate to fill a position or indifferent toward it—information that is normally impossible to come by—has a significant effect on the final outcome. Virtually every situation where I have seen the individual give an answer to "What would it take?" has ended poorly.

The most common reaction to the question is to go high. You might think that the company did ask, so what could possibly go wrong? Almost everything, as it turns out. Shooting high exposes you as being greedy, and far more often than not, abruptly ends negotiations.

This is a lesson that two bond traders learned the hard way when they attempted to extract an absurdly high number from a European investment bank.

"What would it take for us to hire you guys?" asked the head of the bank's trading desk.

Rightfully, the duo should have deflected with the standard "We're here to see if there is a fit" speech. However, I was advising only one of the two, and the other had no idea about my involvement. I had warned my client repeatedly not to give out a number, but his partner in crime felt differently. So, they took a shot at answering the question.

"Five-and-a-half by two by two," they replied.

"Huh?"

"$5.5 million a year for two years for each of us," the pair clarified.

"You realize that adds up to $22 million?" The head of the trading desk wanted to make sure that he had heard right.

"Yes."

"You think that's reasonable?"

"We think so," they replied, refusing to take the hint embedded in that question.

"Let me think about it. I'll call you back," the manager replied. The boot was now on the other foot.

I was furious when I heard what they had done. The trading head was a friend of mine, and I had encouraged him to hire the two traders. Their exorbitant demand, however, had ensured that the matter would go no further.

"What were you thinking?" I scolded my client.

"That's where we see the market," he replied.

"Are you out of your mind?" I snapped. Fortunately, he did not argue. He knew full well that I had negotiated on behalf of several of his fellow traders and, as a result, knew the going rate as well as him, if not better. It gradually dawned on him that they had made a huge mistake.

"Can you ask the bank to come back to the negotiating table? We would like to start again," he said glumly.

I tried, but failed.

"No, Kamal," the trading head said, "We've moved on."

"I'm sure they will agree to a lower number if you want to re-engage."

"Absolutely not! I've seen what these guys are made of, and I have no interest in hiring them," he replied. Even in an industry that thrives on greed, it is considered uncouth to be too greedy.

I gave up. Had the two asked the company for a number first, they would have likely started at three by two by two for a grand total of $12 million. That ship, however, had sailed. Instead, the bank went ahead and hired the next candidate on their list—there is always someone else—for a mere three by one.

Going high in response to "what would it take" almost always terminates the discussion. However, that does not imply that going low is a good idea either. In addition to immediately placing a cap on your pay, it may make managers wonder why you priced yourself this low. Perhaps you are not as good as they thought you were. Besides, since no one ever goes low intentionally, it betrays the fact that you are unaware of your market value. The question therefore arises: What else are you clueless about? Even if the managers were to ignore this possibility, you are still at risk of their quickly agreeing to your number, thereby ensuring years of underpayment. You could still turn the job down, but it is improper to walk away when the other side has agreed to your demands. That is why I do extensive market research and make sure that every client knows the market rate for someone with their skill set and experience.

A very long time ago, I too was clueless about my market value and needed the help of an advisor. At the end of my first year on Wall Street (1993), I would have been happy getting paid a total of $100,000—$60,000 in salary and $40,000 in bonus.

When a colleague of mine heard this, he burst out laughing.

"You should ask for a bonus of $100,000," he said, making my head reel.

"But that would make my total compensation $160,000!"

"Yes, you fool. Just go in there and ask for it."

I had not yet learned the lesson that you always ask the other side for a number first, so I did as he had asked. That year, the company paid me a bonus of $90,000, making my total compensation $150,000. One simple statement from my colleague had netted me an extra $50,000. This experience opened my eyes to the importance of knowing your market value and to the pitfalls of quoting the opening number. My boss had paid me $90,000 because it was slightly lower than what I had asked for. At the time, I didn't have the courage or the self-confidence to shoot for a higher number. It is impossible to know what would have happened if I had asked for an extra $50,000. Would I have gotten paid more, or would my boss have been furious with me? Regardless, this was the last time I quoted the first number in any negotiation.

WHEN THE TACTIC FAILS

I would be remiss if I didn't acknowledge that, once in a while, this approach of mine (insisting that the corporation give out the first number) does not work. I have encountered managers that have reacted negatively to a candidate's refusal to name their price.

"If you won't give us a number, then we won't give you an offer."

My response in these situations is to walk away. Any company that allows managers to bully a potential hire is not worth working for. So, I ask the candidate to respond in kind.

"In that case, I don't think we are a good fit for each other."

This display of resolve on the part of the individual sometimes jolts the managers into submission. And if it doesn't, then it's game over. If a boss sees it fit to indulge in strong-arm tactics *before* the employee has accepted the job offer, I shudder to think how they would behave once they have the person in their clutches. This is a perfect example of a situation where not getting a signed contract is the best possible outcome.

IN CONCLUSION

Every company knows beforehand what it is willing to pay for an open position. Yet, manager after manager still persists with the question, "What would it take?" The only possible explanation that I can come up with is that big business is not satisfied with the immense advantage that it already possesses. It must have more. Therefore, it becomes all the more important to fight the scourge of "What would it take?" by refusing to provide the opening number to any employer. Always remember that when it comes to discussing money, one who moves last moves best.

CHAPTER 3

AN OPENING OFFER IS JUST THAT: AN OPENING

THE MOST SIGNIFICANT aspect of an opening offer is its mere existence, rather than the amount offered. A corporation's initial offer—the first number *must* be quoted by the company—signals that the game has begun, and negotiations can now commence. As with any sporting contest, it is of little consequence where a negotiation begins. What matters is where it ends. Therefore, I consider an opening offer to be nothing more than a starting point for the game to follow. Incidentally, even the company knows that its opening salvo is not the final word. Managers fully expect their chosen candidate to negotiate, and it is incumbent upon you to not disappoint them[4].

As discussed earlier, the words "we'd like to hire you" are a prerequisite for any salary-related negotiation. That simple statement reveals that, at least for the moment, you are the

---

[4] Entry-level positions are usually exempt from this rule.

company's chosen candidate. It is rare for a corporation to offer the same job to more than one candidate simultaneously. What if they both accept? It is far more typical for managers to start from the top applicant on their list and work their way down. If and when it's your turn, you can be reasonably confident that you have the company on the hook and can set about reeling it in.

FROM DEFENSE TO OFFENSE

The opening offer marks a sharp turning point in a candidate's dealings with an employer. Until that moment, the company remains in charge of the hiring process. As soon as a job offer is made, though, the situation is reversed—the individual is now in the driver's seat. While this principle holds true for most business negotiations, it is especially true for employment-related ones. The power mismatch between an individual and a corporation makes it imperative that you play defense until the managers have revealed their cards. Once they have done that, you can subtly but decisively transition to playing offense. This is why I instruct every client to be compliant during the early stages of the hiring process and to do the exact opposite in the second half of the game. Managers are often taken aback by this change in the candidate's demeanor, but it never occurs to them that it was a pre-planned move.

The reason this transition (from defense to offense) works is because large corporations have highly formalized hiring processes that require approval from not only everyone who interviewed the candidate but also from layers of management. Getting all these ducks in a row takes substantial effort on the hiring manager's part and places additional pressure on them to "close" the deal. At this stage, as long as the individual makes reasonable demands—making unreasonable demands is never a good idea—there is every chance that they will be met.

START BY NEGOTIATING JOB DESCRIPTION AND TITLE

Before delving into the financial details of any job offer, I first try to negotiate the precise job description and the title of the position. The objective is to expand one's responsibilities and attain a higher title. Adding "senior" to your business card will not only command more respect within and outside the company, but it will also boost your career prospects. Similarly, having taken on more responsibilities looks better on your résumé and will likely prove crucial in a future job search. For this reason, I often ask prospective managers to hold off on making a formal offer until these two issues have been resolved. I am acutely aware that if I am successful on either or both of these fronts, my client's pay will automatically go up.

At first glance, it seems improbable that you could negotiate the responsibilities of the role or its title. After all, every listing not only outlines a job's function but also its position within the corporate hierarchy. However, most job advertisements only contain the minimum qualifications for the role and do not place an upper limit on a candidate's education or experience. A job that mandates an undergraduate degree does not disqualify someone who has a master's degree. Likewise, a candidate with eleven years' experience is not barred from a job that requires only seven. In both these instances, the more qualified candidate can rightfully make a case for greater responsibilities as well as a higher title. Companies often give in because it is rare to find an exact match for the advertised role, especially in a tight labor market. Time is money in the corporate world, and having a bird in hand is preferable to waiting. I have lost count of the number of times I have been able to successfully add to a client's duties and get them a higher title.

Once you are satisfied with these two aspects of the job, you can turn your attention to its financial terms. It is worth noting that an offer can contain anywhere from five to ten economic components, not all of which are negotiable. Make sure that you focus only on the terms that can be improved and not waste time on those that cannot. There is little to be gained by getting into a fight over an issue where a manager's hands are tied and they counter with "Sorry, it's company policy."

KNOW WHAT IS NEGOTIABLE AND WHAT ISN'T

When dealing with a large corporation, I never try to negotiate benefits such as health insurance, retirement plans, or relocation assistance. Decisions about these aspects are made at a high level in the organization and are applied uniformly across the workforce (except for some very senior executives). There are complex rules that govern how the various plans are administered—make sure you ask for a copy of the relevant documents—and no single manager has the power to change them.

Corporate health plans are referred to as Group Insurance since they apply to the entire group of employees. It would be impossible for a company to customize healthcare individually for each of its workers. Likewise, retirement plans are standard across the company and cannot be individually tailored. The same principle applies to relocation benefits (where applicable) regarding the transportation of an employee's household goods or providing them with temporary accommodation.

Company-wide benefits notwithstanding, as we'll see below, there is plenty in a job offer that is negotiable. However, your first task is to understand the company's compensation structure because not all opening offers are created equal.

UNDERSTAND THE COMPENSATION STRUCTURE

The headline numbers (salary and bonus) in any job offer rarely tell the whole story. While it is too early to delve into the contractual language of the offer, this is the right time to ask pointed questions about its structure, especially as it relates to deferred pay and stock awards.

A standard practice on Wall Street for decades, which is becoming increasingly common for corporations, is to not only postpone a portion of an employee's compensation for several years but also to pay it in company stock. Furthermore, the stock component of the award is sometimes restricted such that the employee is unable to sell it for a specified time period. The failed investment bank, Lehman Brothers, had a policy that prevented employees from selling the company stock for an additional five years *after* it had vested. In the financial crisis of 2008, many Lehman employees saw their stock holdings plummet to zero simply because the five-year lockup had not expired. Even before Lehman's demise, I would have argued against owning significant amounts of your employer's stock. Otherwise, in an economic downturn, you are exposed to the double whammy of not only losing your job but also taking a hit on your portfolio when you can least afford it.

Making matters considerably worse, company policy often requires employees to forfeit their entire deferred compensation upon leaving. That is why I would accept a lower all-cash offer than one that has a higher headline number but is subject to deferral. With the former, you know exactly what you are getting paid, whereas with the latter, it depends upon your tenure at the company. Moreover, deferred pay makes you more expensive— hence, less attractive—for your next employer since they must reimburse you for it.

As abhorrent as deferred pay is, rules governing it are set in stone, and therefore, non-negotiable. Still, you must gain a complete understanding of the compensation framework before turning your attention to the negotiable aspects of the job offer and adjusting them accordingly.

NEGOTIATE THE NEGOTIABLE

The negotiable aspects of a job offer typically consist of salary, annual bonus, stocks and options, and a sign-on incentive. Your goal should be to maximize the total compensation package and not any individual component. While you might be indifferent to which of these you nudge upward, the same cannot be said for most corporations. They often have "buckets" that are allocated to various aspects of employees' compensation. By showing flexibility—"Where do you have room?"—you allow managers to dip into the bucket that fits them best.

Nevertheless, you should start by negotiating for a higher salary and a larger annual bonus. After that, I would focus on stocks and options, and finally, the sign-on bonus. Salary and bonus are recurring payments, and a 10 percent increase in the company's initial offer will likely increase your subsequent years' pay by the same amount. As far as stocks and options go, I place less value on those than I do on salary and bonus. Stocks are inherently risky and stock options even more so. Despite that uncertainty, it is still worth trying to negotiate them upward, especially if they are awarded every year. The same cannot be said for a sign-on bonus, which, by definition, is a one-time payment. Therefore, I try for a sign-on bonus only after I have maximized salary, annual bonus, stock, and options.

However, you shouldn't confine yourself to negotiating just these five elements of a job offer. From time to time, the greatest advantage is derived from unexpected sources.

DON'T OVERLOOK THE UNEXPECTED

I am keenly aware of the negotiable and the non-negotiable components of a job offer, but that does not prevent me from being open to new and creative ways to maximize the pay. As we shall see below, in one instance, it took the form of an ownership stake in the company, while in another, the corporate division of labor led to a significant victory.

It is nearly impossible to anticipate the unexpected ways in which a company can enhance your compensation. These avenues are highly specific to every corporation and unknown to outsiders. However, a well-placed "What can you do?" can often allow you to discover the possibilities that are unique to a company. Furthermore, that question is best posed when negotiations are at a standstill, after you have exhausted the standard elements of your pay package. The key is to remain adaptable and always be on the lookout for an advantage.

"WHAT CAN YOU DO?"

I have resorted to using this open-ended question during several of my own negotiations. In one of those cases, my employer sought to introduce a "clawback" clause in my existing contract, enabling the company to reclaim past compensation if I were to incur trading losses in the future. Despite being in the middle of a 103-month long streak of positive returns, I balked.

"Are you afraid of having a losing year?" my boss asked.

"Not at all," I said.

"Then why don't you sign this?"

"Because you are asking me for something without offering anything in return," I replied.

"What would you like?"

"I'm not sure. What can you do?"

My boss paused for a moment and came up with a stunning proposal.

"Fine, what if we give you a small stake in the company?"

"In that case, I agree," I replied, without skipping a beat.

I didn't waste any time in saying yes because, in that instant, the owner had gone from seeking something for nothing to overpaying for it. This fact was borne out over the next few years, when my ownership stake yielded a six-figure return. The clawback clause, on the other hand, expired, worthless since I remained consistently profitable.

You may have noticed that this negotiation was performed with a current employer and not a future one. However, before I walked into the conference room on that fateful morning, I had decided that I wasn't going to give in. I had gone so far as to type up a resignation letter and placed it in my pocket. If the encounter had turned confrontational, I would have quit on the spot. That mindset allowed me to negotiate from the perspective of an ex-employee rather than an existing one. I am confident that the owner yielded only because it was clear that I was prepared to walk.

EXPLOIT THE CORPORATE DIVISION OF LABOR

A large corporation operates by dividing responsibilities among its employees. That division of labor sometimes leads to situations where an individual finds himself negotiating with multiple parts of the same company. The all-too-common lack of coordination (or even communication) between divisions leaves companies vulnerable to being taken advantage of.

In one such case, a client gained a substantial win because the company decided to outsource the assessment of his deferred compensation. As discussed before, I consider negotiating to be akin to a poker game where the objective is to draw an error from your opponent. By isolating the three components of my client's compensation—salary, bonus, and the buyout of his existing deferred pay—we were able to extract concessions that would have otherwise been impossible.

As planned, John first negotiated his salary and bonus with his prospective manager. The task of valuing his deferred compensation was then assigned to an HR committee which, in turn, sought assistance from an outside specialist. It appeared that no one wanted to take responsibility for the matter, something that occurs frequently in large corporations and proved to be the key to our success.

This matter was passed from person to person because of the unusually complex nature of John's current contract. As a partner at a private equity firm, his pay package consisted of salary, bonus, an ownership stake in the company, annual stock awards that vested over several years, and an interest in the company's various funds, which would also be paid out gradually over time. It was easily the most complicated employment contract that I had ever seen.

Although I was going to insist that the other side come up with a number first, I still wanted to have an idea of what John's deferred compensation was worth. However, instead of focusing on this one aspect of his pay, I aggregated all of its components to determine their present value. When I compared that number to the offer that was currently on the table, I arrived at a startling conclusion. The correct buyout number for his deferred compensation was exactly zero! The jump in his salary and bonus alone was more than enough to compensate him for all of his lost deferral.

John was understandably concerned by the findings of my analysis.

"We are not going to tell them any of this, right?" he said, just to make sure.

"Of course not," I replied, "This will remain between us. Instead, we will make a case that your deferral is worth millions."

We did exactly that. It was a bold move, but I felt that it was justified under the circumstances. It is hard to believe, but no one at the corporation had taken a look at John's overall pay structure. His future manager seemed to not care about deferred compensation since it came from a different bucket. Likewise, HR and their external specialist were not concerned about John's salary and bonus because that bucket belonged to someone else. A week and several pointed conversations with John later—I had prepared him for those via mock sessions—the company came up with an opening number.

"We can pay you $1 million as a buyout of your existing contract."

John was ecstatic. It was an extra million dollars that rightfully did not belong to him. That fact, however, did not prevent him from expressing great disappointment with the number. After all, we had argued that his deferral was worth an order of magnitude more. Given that, accepting *only* $1 million seemed ridiculous.

"I really want to join, but such a steep discount is tough to swallow. Do you have any room in this?"

"Let us see what we can do."

To our great astonishment, the company returned the following week. "The most we can do is $2 million. That's our final number."

"Understood. Let me think about that, and I'll come back."

I doubled over with laughter when I heard this. John, needless to say, was over the moon. The following day he "reluctantly" accepted the company's final offer.

IN CONCLUSION

The most significant aspect of any opening offer is that the company now regards you as a preferred candidate. Start by focusing on the job description and the title before turning your attention to salary, bonus, stocks, options, and a sign-on bonus (in that order). Company-wide benefits, on the other hand, are generally non-negotiable and are best left alone. Furthermore, remain flexible and be on the lookout for unconventional avenues to enhance your total compensation. A straightforward question such as "What else can you do?" often prompts future managers to reveal a pathway that was hidden until now but could ultimately prove highly lucrative.

CHAPTER 4

EVERY WORD MATTERS

WHEN TWO SIDES are engaged in a battle of wits, otherwise known as a negotiation, they have just one weapon at their disposal: words. How this weapon is wielded—both defensively as well as offensively—has a direct impact on the final outcome. A savvy negotiator uses the opponents' words to decipher their hand while making sure that their own words don't betray the strength (or weakness) of their own position. And if at the end of the long, tortuous road—negotiations are rarely short or peaceful—there happens to be a written contract, the negotiator examines every word with a fine-tooth comb.

WORDS CONTAIN A TELL

The exact words used by your opponents matter because there is usually a tell buried somewhere. Poker players are especially mindful of this. In an attempt to get a read on their opponent, they pay careful attention to both the words spoken by their opponent and their physical gestures. As a behind-the-scenes negotiator, I don't have access to the other side's body language. Hence, I ask every client to pay close attention to the exact language used by the opposition and then repeat it to me, word for word. When it comes to emails and text messages, I meticulously examine them for hidden information and draft the responses myself.

However, words by themselves carry little meaning. You must also pay attention to the context in which they are delivered. An angrily blurted "This is our final offer" carries considerably less weight than the same words contained in a careful email drafted by the firm's lawyers. The former can be dismissed as mere bluster while the latter demands respect.

"LET US KNOW WHAT YOU THINK"

You cannot expect a future manager to simply inform you that the company is willing to pay more. Instead, you must look for clues in the words accompanying a proposal to determine if there is room in it. For instance, it is fairly common for an offer or a counteroffer to be accompanied with a friendly "Let us know what you think." At first glance, this casual phrase appears like a polite gesture, but in reality, it serves as an invitation to negotiate. The manager is effectively saying, "This is our current offer, but we are open to a counterproposal from you." So, I would keep pushing until the company says something akin to "This is our best." At that point, you should either accept or reject the offer, and not make another proposition. If it turns out that the company was bluffing, then the managers will come back with an improved offer after you've turned them down.

I know that the sentence "Let us know what you think" indicates a willingness to negotiate because I frequently use it myself. I prefer not to make take-it-or-leave-it proposals during negotiations, so my responses often end with "Let me know what you think." I realize that I am signaling the possibility that my client may accept less than what we've asked for. But that is what negotiating is all about. There have been instances where managers have missed this rather obvious cue and quickly agreed to our latest offer. Contrary to what you might expect, I don't see that as a cause for celebration. It means that we didn't ask for enough in our latest proposal and, as a result, left money on the table. I would much prefer pushing a corporation—gently, if possible, and not so gently, if necessary—as far as I can before accepting *their* offer, rather than having them accept mine. Nonetheless, no matter who does the accepting, I ask every client to abide by the terms that have been agreed to. Needless to say, I insist that every corporation also do the same, which is easier said than done.

NEVER TRUST A "TRUST ME"

Virtually every contract I've reviewed includes a clause stating that the document nullifies any verbal communication between the two parties. Therefore, you must ignore any promise made by a corporation's representatives unless it is put in writing. The words "Trust me" out of a manager's mouth have no value whatsoever. I have known bosses who simply "forgot" that they had made a commitment to an underling. Even if your boss has every intention of honoring their promise, the same cannot be said for their bosses. I have heard the line "It was out of my hands" more often than I care to remember.

I rarely give ultimatums during the early stages of any negotiation, but the converse is true when it comes to the wording of a contract. Unless the language accurately reflects the agreement that was reached, I ask a client to walk away. If a company allows a negotiation to fall apart at this stage, you can be certain that they had no intention of fulfilling the terms of the contract in the first place.

Perhaps no other case illustrates this phenomenon better than the one involving a computer expert looking to become a freelancer. Milos was a Polish immigrant who held a steady, albeit unglamorous, job managing the computer systems of a large New York law firm. After a decade of working at the company, he was considering becoming an independent contractor, primarily to earn more money. However, having spent his entire working life at one company, he didn't know the first thing about being a free agent.

"I make $125,000 a year at the law firm. What do you think I should aim for as a freelancer?" he asked.

"The minimum you need is $125 an hour," I replied.

"But that's double my current hourly rate!"

"Yes, you need the cushion to compensate for the lack of benefits and for the gaps between assignments when you'll be sitting at home, earning nothing," I explained.

"Understood."

As luck would have it, a consulting firm expressed strong interest in hiring Milos for a six-month project at one of its customers. After a series of interviews, including some at the client site, the company offered to pay him $140 an hour. In just six months, he would earn $140,000, with the potential for earning even more in the second half of the year. Milos was thrilled, but I felt it was too early to celebrate.

"Let's wait for the paperwork before we declare victory," I cautioned him.

The contract was delivered the following week, and it stated clearly that he would be paid at the discussed hourly rate, but there was no mention of the six-month term that he had been promised. I told Milos in no uncertain terms that it would be foolish to leave his current job without being guaranteed the run rate for at least a few months. Otherwise, he risked being terminated an hour after he started, with no recourse.

"That makes sense to me. I will ask them to put a six-month term in the contract," he said.

"Good idea!"

What happened next made our heads spin. Even though he was only asking for something that had been verbally agreed upon, the company responded with, "We don't think you are the right person for the job. We plan to go in a different direction." He had been fired before he was even hired.

This is a perfect example of a corporation making promises that it had no intention of keeping. Despite Milos being an excellent fit for the assignment, the consulting company chose to go in a "different direction," which is just another word for a poor sap who won't read the contract too carefully. This brief foray into the world of independent contracting made Milos realize that he was better off staying where he was. He remains there to this day.

CONTRACT LANGUAGE IS ALL-IMPORTANT

While it is far from the endpoint of any negotiation, a verbal agreement is still an important milestone. Whether it is reached on the phone, over email, or via a text message, you should know that the deal (for now) is non-binding. I temper a client's enthusiasm at this stage because there is a significant probability of the negotiations falling apart. First-time clients are often surprised by my circumspect attitude. "We have reached a deal, after all," they assert. "What could possibly go wrong?" A lot, as it frequently turns out.

No corporation has ever allowed an individual to draft a contract. Contracts are prepared exclusively by expensive lawyers whose sole responsibility is to protect the company's interests. Since a contract, much like an employment negotiation, is also a zero-sum game, any clause that is beneficial to the corporation inherently works against the individual. It should, therefore, come as no surprise that I pay a great deal of attention to every word of a contract. In general, I have found that the higher the amounts involved, the more complex the language. I have gone through hundreds of employment contracts over the last three decades and can identify the common pitfalls and get corporations to fix them. Still, I am not a lawyer, and sometimes, especially for high-priced contracts, the task is best left to a professional. When I determine that to be the case, I send the client and their contract to my attorney of 25 years. It is worth noting that the lawyer's only job is to formalize the verbal agreement reached with the company. While lawyers have a free hand in negotiating the language of the various clauses in the contract, they are not permitted to alter the economic terms of the agreement. In other words, the lawyer is not the negotiator.

There are two reasons for this approach. First, I have found that employment lawyers tend to not make good negotiators. Making sure that the words in a contract are legally enforceable is a very different skill from trying to get the most money out of a corporation. Second, lawyers are expensive. It is not uncommon for a run-of-the-mill attorney to charge $500 an hour and for high-powered ones to bill at a significantly higher rate, upward of $1,000 an hour. Consequently, I handle much of the contractual legwork myself before passing the paperwork on to a lawyer.

WATCH OUT FOR DODGY SENTENCES

Perhaps the most egregious example of dodgy language occurred while I was helping a young finance professional negotiate with a prominent hedge fund. In a single sentence, the company gave itself five opportunities to deny the bonus that had been guaranteed to my client, albeit only verbally:

> *You will be eligible for a target discretionary bonus of $300,000, subject to your performance and the firm's profitability.*

First, this sentence makes the individual only "eligible" for the bonus, just as I might be "eligible" to win the Powerball lottery upon purchasing a ticket. Second, the bonus is stated as "target" as well as "discretionary," implying that it is an aspirational number (as opposed to a minimum), which the company is not legally obligated to pay. As bad as this sentence is so far, it adds two more outs for the hedge fund. Even if "your performance" was exemplary throughout the year, the bonus could still be denied if the "firm's profitability" turned out to be lower than expected. Making matters worse, the company refused to define the metrics that would determine the individual's performance or the firm's profitability, thereby making a mockery of the words "guaranteed bonus." I consider this sentence to be a work of legalese art, crafted with the sole purpose of shafting the individual.

I asked my client to confront the hedge fund over this sentence. His future boss admitted that the firm did not offer explicit guarantees, which was the exact opposite of everything he had said until then. My guess is that the company thought that they could slip this language into the contract and the young man would not notice. I asked my client to walk away, but he refused to do so. Against my advice, and to my great disappointment, he signed one of the most awful contracts I have ever seen.

Fortunately, it didn't cost him, at least not monetarily. At the end of the year, the company did pay him the "target discretionary" bonus of $300,000. Despite the fact that everything fell into place for him, I believe that my client played it wrong. He endured eight months of uncertainty, wondering "will they or won't they?" before finally discovering the answer. It turned out to be a cheap lesson that a well-drafted contract provides immense peace of mind.

WORDS ALSO MATTER WHEN YOU GET FIRED

Words are of great consequence not only when you enter a corporation but also when you are on your way out, especially if your exit is involuntary. Getting fired is one of life's more unpleasant experiences, but you must still keep your wits about you and pay close attention to the words of those charged with dismissing you. Likewise, you must be extraordinarily careful with your own words and resist the urge to vent. Getting rid of an employee in a large corporation is a time-consuming process that requires approval from both HR and the legal department. If you get terminated in this manner, you can be certain that the company has acted with great deliberation, so you must do the same. Consequently, it is best to leave quietly without raising a fuss.

A temporary retreat from the battlefield, however, is not the same as an unconditional surrender. What may seem like a lost cause still holds potential for a reasonable outcome, as a client of mine—I'll call him Andrew—discovered. The resolution of that case hinged upon a single sentence uttered by the HR representative as she steered her latest victim out of the building.

I barely knew Andrew on the day that he showed up at my doorstep, looking as if he'd seen a ghost. He had been fired that afternoon, which by itself was hardly newsworthy—someone gets kicked off the Wall Street carousel nearly every day. What made Andrew's dismissal unusual was that the investment bank had fired him *for cause*, the kiss of death in the financial industry.

Cause is a legal term that implies serious wrongdoing on the part of the individual—insubordination, failing a drug test, or sexual harassment, to name a few. The company had ejected Andrew from the premises and threatened to confiscate every dollar he was owed. Losing millions, however, was the least of his troubles. Of far greater concern was the fact that the accusation would become a part of his record. Since any Wall Street person's past can be opened with the click of a mouse, the stigma would follow him for years. Only in his thirties, the poor man was looking down the barrel of a ruined career.

I was shocked to hear this. A dismissal for cause in the financial industry is exceedingly rare. I had witnessed a great deal of wrongdoing during the great financial crisis of 2008; yet, I wasn't aware of a single individual who had been fired in this manner. What had Andrew done that was so much worse? I peppered him with endless questions to figure out the reasons.

The precise reasons for Andrew's dismissal are beyond the scope of this text, but having finally understood them, I concluded that a termination for cause was unjustified. Also, the infraction that led to his dismissal had come to light almost five months earlier. Why had the company not fired him then? The answer, I felt, was fairly straightforward: money. A year ago, the investment bank had lured Andrew from a competitor with a substantial pay package. In return, the company expected their new hire to deliver a stream of trading profits that never materialized. Nevertheless, a typical Wall Street contract is not contingent on performance and the company was required to pay him.

Unless, that is, they fired him for cause.

The invocation of cause would allow the bank to walk away from all its contractual obligations. It wouldn't have to shell out a penny. This is why he had been fired in January, just before bonuses were to be paid. Had he been let go in August, I would have felt differently about the matter.

The burning question in any conflict is this: *Why does the other side fight?* If the bank was acting on principle, then Andrew was in a tough spot. In addition to facing years of expensive litigation, he would be rendered unemployable because of the lawsuit. I took comfort in the fact that in decades of negotiating against large corporations, not once had I seen a company take a stand on principle. It is always about money. If that was the case here too, then the bank's threats were simply an invitation to a negotiation and cause was merely a smokescreen.

The parting shot delivered by the HR representative provided me with a clue to the bank's intentions. Her final comment to my client, as she collected his building pass, was something along the lines of "Let us know what you'd like to do."

Let us know what you'd like to do?

The police do not ask a criminal what *the criminal* would like to do. If the company had truly intended to terminate Andrew with prejudice, they would not have asked him what *he* would like to do. Given that HR is trained to speak with extreme care when firing employees, there was no chance that the comment had been made flippantly or in error. As far as I was concerned, she might as well have said, "How much will you accept?"

I gave Andrew my verdict.

"No one is getting fired for cause. You will settle this matter at 65 cents on the dollar."

He was stunned. Only hours earlier, he had been told in no uncertain terms that his employment was being terminated for cause and that the firm would pay him nothing. And yet, here I was, not only dismissing the threat of cause but also claiming that the company would pay him two-thirds of what he was owed. I wasn't sure if he believed me, but for the first time that day, he had reason for optimism.

It took several weeks and numerous twists and turns—they are elaborated upon in subsequent chapters—but we did ultimately reach a satisfactory resolution. Andrew left the company without the slightest blemish on his record and with more than half of what he was owed.

IN CONCLUSION

Whether you are in the process of getting hired by a corporation or being fired by one, pay careful attention to the language the other side uses. Their choice of words often provides a hint for the negotiation to follow. If and when you reach a verbal agreement with a company, do not rely on a verbal "Trust me" and insist on a well-drafted contract instead. If the document is incomprehensible to you, do not be afraid to utilize the services of a lawyer.

CHAPTER 5

EMPLOY LEVERAGE

"Give me a place to stand, and a lever long enough, and I will move the world."

ALTHOUGH THIS FAMOUS quote by Archimedes is metaphorical and not to be taken literally, it captures the essence of leverage: how a small force, when applied strategically, can influence the behavior of a significantly larger entity. In other words, if you are to have any hope of dislodging a powerful corporation from its entrenched position, you will need to employ leverage. Fortunately, in every case that I have been associated with, the individual has possessed some form of influence, whether or not they realized it. Simply being involved in a negotiation gives you a say in its outcome; otherwise, the opposing side wouldn't waste time arguing with you. The key is to identify the source and scope of your leverage. Knowing how much pressure to apply is just as critical as knowing where and when to apply it. Using more force than is necessary runs the risk of a negotiation coming apart at the seams. So, exercise caution and stay within your limits even as you press your advantage home.

A JOB OFFER IS LEVERAGE

The existence of a job offer implies that the individual has gained the upper hand. As previously noted, most large corporations have elaborate hiring procedures that require candidates to clear a series of hurdles. The time and effort invested during the interview process causes the company to become vested in the winner of the race. The pressure is now on the corporation, or rather, its representatives, to ensure that the successful candidate signs on the dotted line and turns into an employee. Consequently, a job offer leads to a notable softening in a future manager's tone, thereby affirming that the tables have indeed turned. That is not to say that negotiations won't turn heated, but that is a topic for a later chapter.

For now, you should rest assured in the knowledge that the company is not hiring you out of charity. It needs something from you. Corporations employ people to either help increase their bottom line (product developers, salespeople) or to preserve it (support staff, HR, legal). Take Google for instance. In the fourth quarter of 2023, the company generated an astonishing $1.96 million in revenue per employee while paying them on average approximately a *tenth* of that amount. That yawning gap between revenue and pay leaves a fair amount of room for negotiation. Even if the company were to magically double every employee's pay—an unthinkable proposition if there ever was one—its profit margin would still remain a healthy 20 percent, down from its lofty 30 percent. Google, incidentally, is not alone. Some variation of this basic fact holds true for every corporation, which is why they are willing to negotiate with you.

PIT COMPANIES AGAINST EACH OTHER

Arguably, the most effective way to leverage your position is to play companies off against each other. I have employed this tactic countless times over the past quarter-century, and with great success. Many of my first-time clients have struggled with playing this high-stakes poker game against not one but two opponents simultaneously. A few have told me, "I gave them my word, and my word is my bond," which makes me laugh. Their initial reluctance notwithstanding, each of those individuals eventually relented and forced companies to compete with each other.

In some cases, a client has played the game simultaneously against not two but three counterparties, going so far as to sign a contract with one company only to resurface at another (after leaving their current job). In a particularly dramatic situation, I once hijacked a Citigroup trader from a taxi as he made his way to Morgan Stanley. I felt strongly that it was in his best interests to join Lehman Brothers instead and convinced him to change course mid-ride. Years later, with his career now in full swing, he would admit, "Kamal saved me." It is worth noting that not one of these individuals suffered any consequences for spurning a corporation even after signing on the dotted line.

In another case, I pitted two investment banks against each other in a tussle over a bond trader. Goldman Sachs (GS) targeted a Credit-Suisse (CS) trader to jump start its flailing trading desk. The moment CS heard that its archrival was attempting to poach a valued employee—I had instructed the trader to deliberately leak this information to his bosses—the company went into overdrive. When the dust had settled, my client had secured a guarantee from CS that was nearly *four* times what GS had offered. Although outcomes of this magnitude are rare, there is still an advantage to be gained by putting companies in competition against each other. After all, that's exactly what they do with us. What's sauce for the goose is sauce for the gander.

As effective as this strategy has proven, I would advise against using it repeatedly with the same counterparty. Your bosses may give in once, but they are loath to make a habit of it lest it encourage other employees to follow suit. A client of mine successfully used a competitor's offer to wrangle a two-year contract from his current employer. Two years later, when he tried the same trick again, he found himself escorted out of the building.

KNOW YOUR LIMITS

No matter how great your advantage during a negotiation, you must still proceed with caution. Even the best starting hand in Texas Hold'em, a pair of aces, doesn't always win. Thus, seasoned poker players tread carefully even when they know that the odds are in their favor. Likewise, shrewd negotiators know to press their advantage only so far. For example, as discussed earlier, firm-wide benefits are generally non-negotiable, so it is best to leave them alone. For the negotiable elements of your compensation, make sure that your response falls in the range of what is possible. Otherwise, the other side will simply walk away, as happened with the two bond traders who were negotiating with a European bank (Chapter 2). The traders held a considerable advantage in the situation, but they still managed to botch the negotiation by asking for too much.

There is another limit that I frequently run into: that of my client. In many negotiations, I find myself having to push the individual further than they are initially willing to go, and at times, even beyond what they thought was possible. Despite that, the individual often ends up accepting less than what I am aiming for. Regardless, whenever a client says, "This is enough," I stop negotiating. They have reached their limit, and attempting to push any further would be unproductive.

CONSIDER THAT YOU MIGHT BE WRONG

Another reason to be careful is that you might have misjudged the situation. As with any game of incomplete information, you can never know your opponent's position with certainty. There are exceptions to this rule, as we shall see in a later chapter, but those are rare and cannot be counted upon. Therefore, I always consider the possibility that I could be wrong and proceed accordingly. Despite that, there have been times when my client and I have misread the state of affairs and caused the negotiation to go off the rails.

One of those cases involved a long-standing client of mine, Kevin, who had received a job offer from a small financial firm. Much like we had done with all our prior negotiations, we dismissed the opening offer as too low and asked the company to improve.

"How far off are we?" the hiring manager asked, which was a reasonable question.

"Very."

In hindsight, we should have been gentler with our reply, if for no other reason than to keep the game going. Instead, our reply ensured that we didn't hear anything back for almost two weeks, the equivalent of a lifetime during a negotiation. In the meantime, there were changes at Kevin's workplace that made him desperate to leave the company. As a result, we found ourselves in a truly awkward position. My client wanted to accept an offer that, unfortunately, was no longer on the table.

"How do we get those guys back?" Kevin asked.

"I'm not sure," I replied.

It took a great deal of effort, but we managed to resuscitate the negotiation. With our tails between our legs, we went back to the future manager and asked for his forgiveness. The manager had labeled my client as a gold-digger and wanted to see real contrition before moving forward. I am not sure how remorseful Kevin really was, but he managed to convey the appropriate sentiment. To our great surprise, the company not only returned to the negotiating table but also improved the offer slightly. Needless to say, it was gratefully accepted.

Kevin was lucky. Once it is derailed, a negotiation may never get back on track. That doesn't mean that you can't say no to a company's latest proposal, but make sure that you do so only after careful deliberation.

Another mistake I have observed, although not from any of

my clients, is employees giving ultimatums to their bosses. In a corporation, no one is indispensable, be they the janitor or the CEO, and everyone can be replaced. Even if managers capitulate to your threats in the short run, they will make sure you pay the price down the road. In one instance, a boss became so incensed at the individual's continued demands that he scuttled her move to another division. She had not realized that an internal transfer required the approval of both bosses, and it cost her dearly in the end. Having greatly misjudged her leverage, she was forced to depart from the company.

RETAIN LEVERAGE EVEN WHEN YOU GET FIRED

Being fired from a job is never a pleasant experience. A quarter-century ago, I too found myself at the receiving end of the "Your time at this company has come to an end" speech from my supervisors. Even though I had seen my firing coming from a mile away and had already secured another job, it still felt like a gut-punch. I would have preferred to quit on my terms (which I would have done the following day) instead of being shown the door by HR.

The trauma that I experienced, however, paled in comparison to that endured by Andrew in the previous chapter. You will recall that he had been fired for cause, a rare but devastating form of termination that had the potential to end his career. Despite the company's claims to the contrary, I not only dismissed the threat of cause but also claimed that he would collect two-thirds of what he was owed. I based my conclusions partly on a comment made by the HR representative earlier in the day and partly because of the leverage that every fired employee retains over the corporation that dismisses them.

On the surface, it would appear that a fired employee has no cards to play. The company, after all, has made it clear that it doesn't want anything further to do with the employee. Nevertheless, every terminated employee has an ace in the hole, something that a corporation needs from them: a release absolving the establishment of any wrongdoing. In my experience, companies require that everyone, especially its discards, sign that document before walking out the door. Otherwise, there is the risk of getting sued or worse, a whistle getting blown. I have often used that release, or rather, my client's refusal to sign it, as a bargaining chip to extract concessions from their soon-to-be ex-employer. In such situations, the company has been willing to pony up substantial amounts in exchange for a duly executed release. During my tenure in the financial industry, I have witnessed some truly egregious conduct. Yet, in every case, the individual was allowed to leave quietly, without a mark on their record. Therefore, I was convinced that the investment bank would settle with Andrew as well. The company's lawyers did not make it easy, though. The hard-fought battle lasted for weeks and, as we shall see in the next chapter, required us to call their bluff when they made a "final" offer.

THERE IS HOPE IN HOPELESS SITUATIONS

Even when the situation appears hopeless, I keep searching for an advantage. I have often found that there is usually a single thread that, once identified and pulled, can cause your adversary to unravel. In one instance, it was the company's failure to share one item of information with my client (as they were legally required to do). It was impossible to know whether the omission had been an honest mistake or an intentional act. Nevertheless, I pounced on it as evidence of our opponent's wrongdoing, driving that point home relentlessly in email after email. There must have been some skeletons in the company's closet because it capitulated shortly thereafter.

In another case, after my client had been turned down by firm after firm, I was forced to use his family connections—an uncle of his was a highly placed official at a large customer. As soon as that fact was revealed, companies that had said no to him found a way to get to yes, likely hoping to leverage his relationship for more business and greater profits. In case you are wondering, I feel no shame in resorting to such tactics. I am willing to exploit any legal advantage that can help a client procure a better deal.

Not all of my efforts are successful. Sometimes, despite all my attempts, I am unable to find an opening. In that case, I simply fold my hand. My surrenders, however, are rarely unconditional. Even as I lay down my arms, I retain a modicum of leverage. There is every chance that my opponent, basking in the glow of victory, might make concessions that they otherwise wouldn't have. So, I keep fighting until the ink is dry on the contract.

WHEN DEFEAT LOOMS

In any game, losing is an unavoidable fact of life. No matter how great your advantage or how hard you try, you are bound to encounter negotiations that are unwinnable. Whether it is the result of your being dealt a lousy hand or having misread the other side's cards, you must learn to lose gracefully. Still, I don't treat any loss as a lost cause. Instead of giving in unconditionally, I try to engineer a negotiated surrender. You will be surprised at how often the victors yield even after they know that they have won.

Strategic capitulation, as I see it, is the act of throwing yourself at your opponent's mercy while also seeking a final concession from them. Even though the strategy appears to be fundamentally illogical—wave the white flag with one hand and ask for more with the other—I have successfully employed it in a wide range of situations. A New York car dealer once gave my client money back because he "felt bad" about his customer being unhappy with the purchase. A logistics company in South India boosted an engineer's pay after he said, "I will agree, but I think my pay is below the market rate. I would feel a lot better if the discount was a little less." Earlier in this chapter, Kevin's capitulation netted him a higher offer *after* he had indicated that he would accept the original terms. Even the smallest of gains at this stage is a win.

Sometimes, though, the boot is on the other foot, and I find myself at the receiving end of such a capitulation. As stated previously, I would much rather accept a corporation's final offer than to have them acquiesce to my latest counterproposal. From time to time, however, my offers do get accepted, and with conditions. In those scenarios, I ask the client to accede to the company's requests as long as they are small. It is just as important to win graciously as it is to lose graciously. In one case, all the corporation wanted was an earlier start date, and in another, to alter the mix of salary and bonus. In the former, I asked the client to agree despite his desire for a longer break between jobs. In the latter, I figured out that the readjustment would actually increase my client's overall pay ever so slightly. So, we consented to the company's request, reluctantly of course.

I do not consider any of this behavior to be altruistic, just good business. It makes sense to keep a counterparty happy, especially after you have emerged victorious. You never know when you might need them again.

💡 IN CONCLUSION

You cannot overcome a powerful corporation without employing some sort of leverage. Luckily, a job offer in itself is evidence of your having gained the upper hand. Exploit that advantage by pitting companies against each other, while also being mindful of the fact that you might have misjudged the situation. If you get fired from a job, use the company release to negotiate better terms for your exit. And when all else fails, capitulate, but ask for something in return. You might just get it.

CHAPTER 6

FIGURE OUT THEIR CARDS AND CALL THEIR BLUFF

FIGURING OUT YOUR opponent's cards is rarely enough to win at poker. You must also consider how the other side views your hand. And it doesn't stop there. The question then becomes what they believe you think about their hand, and so on. The complexity quickly escalates to the point where you find yourself standing between two mirrors, not knowing which way to turn. It is for this reason that the best hand doesn't always win in poker, but the better player usually does. The same is true for a negotiation, where the side with the best position doesn't necessarily prevail.

When trying to figure out a company's cards, I tend to go as far as the second or third step but with one key difference. I also try to figure out how my opponent feels about their own hand. A manager with a weak hand who (mistakenly) believes that they are playing from a position of strength needs to be dealt with very differently than one who understands the shortcomings of their position. The same holds true when I face a manager who holds a strong hand but is unaware of it as opposed to one who is fully aware. Otherwise, I run the risk of ending up like the gambler who blames their loss on their opponents' incompetence. It is worth noting that this approach is not equivalent to thinking two or three moves ahead. All of this contemplation occurs at one moment in time: when it is my turn to move. If I am convinced that the company's representatives understand that their position is weak, I ignore their threats and call their bluff.

DON'T GIVE IN TO PRESSURE

A friend of mine, Dev, discovered this uncomfortable fact when trying to hire a former colleague. Dev had just changed jobs, and I helped him secure an excellent deal from his new employer. Shortly after starting at the company, he tried to recruit his former assistant who, in turn, asked me for help. Rachel had seen me negotiate for several of her former colleagues, and she assumed that I would do the same for her. Seeing this as yet another case of a young person battling a powerful corporation, I was only too happy to help.

A natural side effect of my negotiating for others is that the line between a client and an opponent frequently gets blurred. It is not unusual for me to negotiate for someone one day and against them the next. I don't see any contradiction in this. Whenever a former client turns into a hiring manager, which is a common occurrence, I have no hesitation in assisting the individual they are planning to hire. Almost always, though, the former clients have no idea that they are dealing with their former advisor.

Dev, unfortunately, turned out to be the exception to that rule. He felt that Rachel's stubbornness was out of character and concluded that it had to be someone else's doing. He didn't have to look far to find the likely culprit.

"Are you helping Rachel negotiate?" he asked me over lunch.

"Yes," I replied, making this the only instance where I have admitted my involvement in a case to an opponent.

"Why?"

"What do you mean why? This is what I do, and you should know that better than anyone else."

"Yes, but now you are screwing me," he said angrily.

"I'm doing no such thing. All I am trying to do is to get her the best possible deal from your company. You just happen to be in the middle," I tried to explain.

"Well, it feels awfully personal to me!"

"I am sorry you feel that way, but that doesn't change anything."

"Fine, since you are her negotiator," Dev was practically shouting now, "I can tell you that this is our best and final offer. We will not pay her a penny more."

"In that case, I can give you her answer right now," I replied calmly. "She will not accept it."

Dev had let his anger get the better of him, and he left the restaurant in a huff. His display of emotion notwithstanding, I was convinced that he was bluffing. He and Rachel had worked together for the past three years, and I couldn't imagine him taking a risk on someone else over a small amount of money. Luckily, Dev too came to this realization the following day and offered to pay her more. This time, Rachel gladly accepted.

While it's useful to figure out a company's cards and call their bluff when you are getting hired, it becomes absolutely vital to do so when you are being fired. Perhaps no other case illustrates this phenomenon more clearly than the ongoing saga of Andrew's termination for cause.

TERMINATIONS OFTEN REQUIRE AN ATTORNEY

When you get terminated by a corporation, make sure that you do not interact with any employee of the company until after your separation agreement is signed. Instead, hire a lawyer and have them represent you for hammering out the details of your dismissal.

Once Andrew had finished narrating the events leading up to his firing, I read him my standard Miranda warning—*anything you say to anyone at the company will be used against you during the negotiation.* Consequently, every communication, no matter how insignificant, had to go through a lawyer. I was just in time too. His boss had been trying to reach him all afternoon, most likely to assert his innocence and to claim that the matter was out of his hands. No doubt he also wanted to sniff out Andrew's planned course of action and pass that information along to the company's lawyers.

Even though it was late on a Friday evening, I managed to track down my attorney. Ted was a seasoned employment lawyer who had handled not only my affairs for the past 15 years but also those of many of my clients. He agreed to represent Andrew as well.

READ THE OPPONENT'S CARDS

From the outset, I had dismissed the investment bank's threats of firing Andrew for cause and paying him zero. I had done so knowing full well that giving out false hope is just about the worst thing a negotiator can do. At the same time, I believe that it serves no purpose to paint the situation as being more dire than it really is.

Despite having spent only a short time on the matter, I had little doubt that the bank would settle with Andrew. I had read the company's cards and found them to be weak. For starters, the bank could ill afford a scandal so quickly after the 2008 financial crisis, which had left the company's reputation in tatters. Moreover, it remains an unfortunate fact that Wall Street management routinely sweeps wrongdoing under the rug for fear of their own complicity coming to light. Compared to the mismarking of securities, front-running of clients, and pre-arranged trading—all violations that I had seen swept under the carpet—Andrew's infraction was insignificant. There was no way he would be the first person I knew who would be fired for cause.

Fortunately for my client, I turned out to be right on all counts. As soon as Ted called the bank, the company indicated that it was willing to discuss a settlement in exchange for Andrew's signature on the all-important release.

DON'T EXPECT IT TO BE EASY

Just because you've read the other side's cards accurately, it doesn't mean that you've won. There is still a battle to be fought, as turned out to be the case here.

Over the next six weeks, using Ted as a go-between, we went back and forth with Andrew's soon-to-be ex-employer. The bank's willingness to negotiate notwithstanding, the company's lawyers went out of their way to make the process as painful as possible. To get even the smallest concession from them was like pulling teeth. I couldn't fault them for this because, in their shoes, I would have done the same. The goal in any negotiation is not to make things easier for your opponent but to frustrate them. I have seen plenty of instances where one side capitulated simply because they'd had enough. It was clear that the bank's lawyers were following the same strategy in the hope that Andrew would cave.

RECOGNIZE A BLUFF

The matter came to a head six weeks later when the bank delivered a "final" offer to our lawyer.

"Forty cents on the dollar," said Ted.

"That's it?" I asked.

"Yes," Ted nodded, "and this is their best and final offer. They are giving us four days to accept. If not, they'll fire Andrew for cause the day after."

"Yeah, right!" I burst out laughing. As far as I was concerned, that ship had sailed a long time ago.

No one else in the conference room was amused. The lawyer, as was his wont, took the threat seriously, and so did Andrew.

Ted continued, "We have three options: accept their offer, come up with a counterproposal, or tell them that we'll see them in court. What do you ..."

"No, we don't. There is a fourth option." I said, cutting him off.

"What's that?"

"We won't even call them back. Let their bullshit deadline pass," I said.

The look of horror on Ted's face was priceless. This option didn't exist in a lawyer's playbook.

"What will that accomplish?" he asked.

Oftentimes, the inflection point in a negotiation—the moment that changes everything—is only revealed in hindsight. On that day, however, it was clear to me that this was it. We had arrived at the make-or-break moment of the battle. And I had come prepared to fight.

"I am sick and tired of this cat-and-mouse game. The company is bluffing. They are in no position to fire anyone for cause. They could have fired Andrew when this matter first came to light, but they chose not to. They threatened again to fire him in January, but they didn't. How on earth can they fire him for cause in March? If Andrew is guilty of serious wrongdoing, why have they offered to pay him 40 percent of his contract? A jury would laugh at them. The company will never allow this matter to reach a court of law because they can't afford the negative publicity. I am willing to bet that the bank needs this matter settled more than Andrew does. Every single one of their threats, deadlines, and ultimatums is a bluff," I exclaimed, fed up with the state of affairs.

CALLING A BLUFF IS A HIGH-RISK MOVE

On the surface, disregarding an ultimatum appears to be a passive act since it involves sitting still. In reality, however, ignoring a threat of this nature is just about the most aggressive move one can make. When the other side delivers a final warning, the last thing they expect is for it to be ignored. The key to a successful negotiation is keeping your opponent off-balance, and this non-move does exactly that. Much like a gambler *on tilt*, an unsteady adversary is prone to making errors.

It is, however, vital to judge your opponent's position accurately while deploying this high-risk tactic, as the consequences of failure are likely to be catastrophic. If I had the slightest doubt about where the bank stood, I would have recommended a far more defensive course of action.

Ted deliberated for a short while before replying.

"Andrew, I have known Kamal for a long time. He negotiates very aggressively. He usually wins, but most people don't have the stomach for it."

The lawyer had hit the nail on the head. I have long believed that it is impossible to win in a negotiation without a stiff dose of courage. It is essential to hold your nerve, no matter how dire the circumstances or how high the stakes.

The stakes for Andrew could not have been any higher. His entire future was on the line. He would either win millions or he would lose everything. Since he was the one who would have to live with the repercussions, the final decision had to be his.

Andrew went into deep thought as he weighed the pros and cons of the various options. To my surprise, and even though it went against his instincts, he decided to go for it.

"Fine, let's not call them back."

I was impressed with his resolve. The choice could not have been easy to make. Ted was uneasy about this course of action, but he agreed to give the company the silent treatment.

Now that the move had been made, it was my turn to feel stressed. Negotiations are inherently unpredictable, and even the best-laid plans can go awry. I had scoffed at the company's latest offer, but it was still a substantial amount of money. Moreover, a settlement would have allowed Andrew to resign from the company, thereby removing the threat of cause. All of these advantages would be lost if I had miscalculated. As always, I kept my fears to myself. My client had enough on his mind.

COMPANIES DO CAPITULATE

The next four days were nerve-racking. The fifth day, the day of reckoning, was particularly stressful as we looked for signs of Andrew having been fired. I breathed a little easier when no such paperwork had been filed by the end of the sixth day either.

Shortly thereafter, Goliath capitulated.

The bank realized that Andrew wasn't going to roll over easily. The company's lawyers called Ted with a higher offer and without an attached ultimatum. They had been bluffing all along. Andrew was ecstatic. I was relieved.

Now that we had the company exactly where we wanted, negotiations moved swiftly forward. In short order, the bank upped its offer to over 50 cents on the dollar, and I began to wonder if two-thirds was too low. Maybe we could take them for even more. Andrew, on the other hand, had had enough. For two months, the threat of cause had hung like the sword of Damocles over him. He just wanted the matter to be settled.

"I think this is enough, Kamal. I'm going to accept."

Even though I felt strongly that he could have gotten more, I didn't stand in his way. In virtually every negotiation, I allow the individual to make the final decision. There are, however, exceptions to this rule as Andrew would see for himself a few weeks later.

The settlement papers were drawn up, and both parties signed them without any fuss, bringing the matter to a close. It had taken months, but Andrew left the company with his head held high and without the slightest blemish on his record.

REFUSAL TO ENGAGE CAN ALSO BE A BLUFF

Not long after the Andrew affair, I found myself in a similar battle against a large financial institution. This time, though, there was no mention of cause, and the terminated individual had been offered $200,000 as settlement. My client, however, felt strongly that her dismissal was unfair and only a larger compensation would allow her to maintain her dignity. Once again, the corporation's lawyers attached an expiration date to their offer.

"The company is giving you three weeks to accept the offer. After that, it will be off the table," her attorney said.

As with the ultimatum in Andrew's case, I did not take this deadline seriously either. To me, it was reminiscent of a department store sign that said, "Sale ends today!" even though another was likely to begin the day after. Moreover, my client in this case was a woman. While corporations routinely fire female employees, they are also wary of being at the wrong end of a discrimination lawsuit. I am willing to exploit an advantage wherever I can find it. If that happens to be my client's gender, then so be it.

We decided to ignore the company's ultimatum and allowed not three, but four weeks to pass. That prompted the company's lawyers to call with a false sense of concern.

"We haven't heard back from you. Hope everything is okay. Do let us know if you need more time."

Unfortunately, my client was in no position to discuss a settlement at the time. She needed some complicated personal issues—that are beyond the scope of this book—resolved first. Since acknowledging that fact would have weakened her negotiating position, I felt that maintaining radio silence was the best option. Our strategy risked making the company angry, but that was a risk I was willing to take.

Two months later, with the personal issues behind her, we were ready to return to the negotiation. The company, however, refused to engage.

"We are not interested in a settlement anymore. You took too long."

"Yeah, right," I laughed.

"What are we going to do?" my client asked.

I was certain that the company was bluffing. Nevertheless, we still needed to find a way to entice them back to the negotiating table. I saw only one way forward.

"Let's go back and tell them that we will accept $400,000."

My client was incredulous. "What makes you think that will work? Didn't they just tell us that they are out?"

"I know what they said, but that's just their anger talking. For three months now, they've been worried about a lawsuit. What other reason could you possibly have for not responding to their offer? I expect cooler heads to prevail once they see a number that finally gets them out of this jam."

I knew that I was taking a gamble, but not a long shot one. More importantly, I saw no other way out of our predicament. I had also calibrated the number to be high enough to invite a counteroffer. The company's lawyers weren't stupid. They knew that $400,000 was just a starting point and that we would accept a lower amount.

I was pleasantly surprised when the company came back with a revised offer that was between our two numbers. A couple of back-and-forth sessions later, the two sides came to a quick agreement. This time, though, having learned their lesson, the company's lawyers gave my client only a handful of days to sign the document. She happily did so and walked away with all her troubles behind her.

IN CONCLUSION

Any game of imperfect information requires you to intuit the other side's hand and figure out how they feel about the relative strength of their position. You should remember that companies bluff routinely, especially when they are firing an employee. If you find your job terminated, the first thing is to get an attorney—sometimes their exorbitant fees are worth it—and then ignore the company's threats and ultimatums. Companies will pay handsomely for a release that absolves them of any wrongdoing, so make sure that you charge them for it.

CHAPTER 7

CREATE A NARRATIVE

A NEGOTIATOR KNOWS that they need to provide a compelling reason to convince the other side to adopt their position. While a logical, well-reasoned argument might help get the point across, I have found that a story proves much more effective. By connecting with the listener on an emotional level, a story can leave a lasting impression that facts alone cannot achieve. Consequently, the better the story, the greater the probability of success. Sometimes, the narrative that accompanies a proposal becomes more significant than the proposal itself. A bitter pill goes down much easier if it is coated with sugar.

Surprisingly, a story need not be accurate—bluffing and misdirection are essential aspects of negotiating—but it must *sound* believable. Nevertheless, as we shall see in a later chapter, I am strongly opposed to lying to mislead an opponent. Creating a story does not mean that you get to create facts.

The story doesn't have to be long. In fact, the shorter it is, the better. A long-winded narrative only serves to make the other side suspicious. It took all of three words—"Just do it"—for one of the greatest marketing campaigns to tell Nike's story. The short phrase captures the essence of what every individual feels while exercising, while also inspiring them to get off the couch and to "just do it." It is impossible to know if Nike's slogan caused more people to go to the gym, but there is no doubt that when it came to buying the company's products, millions of people "just did it." The story most definitely made the sale.

NEGOTIATING IS MARKETING

A negotiation, in essence, serves as a marketing campaign for your point of view. If you hope to make the sale, you need to learn how to spin a story. Nike's slogan says nothing about the virtues of the company's shoes. Yet, it functions effectively as a battle cry for nearly every aspect of life. Likewise, "Got milk?" successfully conveys the message that life is incomplete without milk. It is difficult to argue that an ad describing the health benefits of milk instead would have worked better.

Even landing a job can often hinge upon an individual's ability to tell a story. During an interview, an open-ended question such as "Why are you the best person for the job?" is an invitation for you to tell your story. Of all the qualified candidates, the one with the most compelling narrative is most likely to win.

In Chapter 1, I had anticipated that Thomas would be asked whether his long absence from the industry would impair his ability to do the job. He could have replied by pointing to his past accomplishments, but that would have been akin to discussing the nutritional value of milk. Instead, I felt that a short narrative about his skills being timeless would be more effective.

"There is only one right way to value securities, and there is only one right way to interact with clients. I knew it then, and I know it now. It makes no difference how much time has passed."

The managers were captivated by how Thomas had managed to capture the essence of the job in one sentence, and they decided to overlook the multi-year gap in his résumé. That short slogan—"I knew it then, and I know it now"— allowed him to beat all the other horses in the race, including many who were currently employed and thus well versed in the state of the market—something Thomas lacked.

TO THE EXTENT POSSIBLE, STICK TO THE FACTS

As impressive as it sounded, Thomas's story was only partly true and could have been debunked by a sharp observer. Despite the risks involved, I felt that the move was necessary given the relative weakness of his position. He got away with it, but that is not always the case. Consequently, to the extent possible, it is best to stick to a narrative that is true and logic that is irrefutable.

During one of my early jobs in the hedge fund industry, I was employed without a contract. As a result, my annual compensation was at the sole discretion of my bosses. Toward the end of my first year, my boss asked me the all-important question.

"What do you think you should get paid?"

"What are you thinking?" I replied, having wizened up to not giving out the opening number.

"I am thinking 10 percent of your profits."

"I think that's too low," I said, which was always going to be my answer.

"What do you think is fair?"

"15 percent."

I was asking for a 50 percent increase in my pay, which is a tall order in any negotiation.

"No one else in the group gets anywhere close to that," he countered.

"That makes perfect sense to me," I quickly replied.

"Why?"

I had come prepared with a story.

"Because I don't need anything from you. Everyone else makes money from the balance sheet that is provided by the bank and allocated by you. I, on the other hand, use hardly any resources and am completely independent."

Everything I had said was true, and if my boss didn't know it before, he knew it now. More importantly, he knew that I knew. I had purposefully omitted my track record—12 straight months of profit—from my story because that would have been akin to pointing out the protein content of milk. Instead, I chose to highlight the one thing that made me different from everyone else at the firm. Moreover, my slogan—"I don't need anything from you"—also contained the implicit threat that I was a free agent who could walk at a moment's notice. As noted earlier, I am not a fan of making explicit threats because doing so paints you into a corner.

That short monologue did its job, and I got paid close to what I had asked for. That jump in pay not only persisted throughout my tenure at the company but also established a baseline for my negotiations with every subsequent employer. I believe that my lifetime earnings would be considerably lower had I not forcefully pushed back that day. Such is the power of a good story.

IF NECESSARY, CREATE A STORY

In this battle between individuals and corporations, I have no hesitation in fabricating a narrative if necessary. I believe that it is up to the company's managers to figure out whether or not the story is accurate. Before you develop a sense of moral outrage about this, you would do well to remember that companies routinely mislead both their employees and their customers. Managers will tell you how valuable you are one day, only to lay you off the next. Sometimes, corporate falsehoods can even have life-and-death consequences, as was the case with Boeing's 737 Max airplane.

Nevertheless, your story must sound believable, and to achieve that, it must contain a kernel of truth. In one case, I seized upon my client's undergraduate major—communications—to argue that she would be a natural fit for an investor relations role. Left unsaid was the fact she had never worked in a similar capacity in the decade since graduation. In another instance, I instructed a friend to emphasize his long tenure in the financial industry as proof of his investing acumen. Despite lacking any experience in managing money or a track record to speak of, Neil still managed to convince a top hedge fund to hire him as a portfolio manager. Not surprisingly, he had a rocky start at his new job, but as we shall see in a later chapter, things eventually worked out for him.

Of all the questions that you are likely to face during an interview, there is one that necessitates a misdirection: "Why are you looking for a job?"[5] An honest answer, such as "I don't get along with my boss" or "I want to get paid more money," is more likely to hurt your cause than to help it. The former paints you as difficult and the latter as greedy. More importantly, they alert your future bosses to the possibility of their facing similar problems with you in the future. Since a successful marketing campaign accentuates the positive and minimizes the negative, you would be much better off providing high-minded responses, such as "Your firm has an incredible reputation, and I'd like to work with the best in the industry" or "I am looking for a new challenge." If you are currently working for a small company and interviewing with a large one, then you can point to a desire to "play in the big league." If the reverse is true, then your answer can be, "I am tired of being a cog in a giant wheel and am looking for a position that will allow me to make a difference." If the two corporations are of similar sizes, then use something that distinguishes one from the other. Just like competing car washes that market themselves as "completely hands-free" or as "hand wash only," you can either be a fan of a company's "strong emphasis on technology" or admire the fact that they "put employees ahead of computers."

In early 2005, while interviewing with a British hedge fund, I purposefully omitted the fact that I was convinced that my current employer was a house of cards that could collapse at any moment. First, no one would have believed that one of the

---

[5] A fresh graduate is usually exempt from this question.

largest Swiss banks was in imminent danger of going under. Second, and more important, that assertion would have marked me as an alarmist and a potential whistleblower, qualities that no employer finds desirable. So, I responded with, "I am looking for a new job because I am tired of having a portion of my pay deferred for several years." My answer was preposterous, but it contained an element of truth. The Swiss bank did defer a part of my bonus, enough for the hedge fund to hire me as their first employee in the United States. The irony was that shortly thereafter, my new employer instituted a deferred compensation policy of their own.

The inescapable conclusion, therefore, is that no manager expects the truth in response to that question. So, don't disappoint them—make something up.

KNOW YOUR AUDIENCE

A storyteller knows that not every story works on everyone. It is crucial, therefore, to adapt your narrative to suit its target audience. Otherwise, you risk offending the very person that you are trying to impress. Thus, it is best to stick to professional matters during an interview and steer clear of sociopolitical issues. Nevertheless, if you feel strongly about a work-related subject, then feel free to express that opinion. I have never shied away from controversy during interviews, especially on topics where my understanding is deeper than that of the interviewer.

Three decades ago, I was merciless on Lehman Brothers' traders as they quizzed me about blackjack. Even if it risked antagonizing my interrogators, I insisted that there was only one right way to play the game, and that wasn't up for debate.

Despite my aggressive posture, or perhaps because of it, I walked off the Lehman trading floor with a job offer in hand.

Years later, I would adopt a similar stance when it came to questions about financial markets. A decade of thought and experimentation had convinced me that there was only one strategy that would lead to long-term success. Nevertheless, when it came to rebutting some of the other more popular methods in the market, I adopted a two-tiered approach. If my interviewer was knowledgeable about the issues involved, I would provide a detailed and thoughtful explanation for why I believed those strategies were unsound. However, I took the opposite approach when trying to raise money for a startup hedge fund, telling potential investors, "I think our time would be better spent discussing strategies that I follow rather than the ones that I don't." In that situation, I knew that my explanation would have been incomprehensible to the audience which, in turn, might have caused them to tune me out—a cardinal sin in any interview. My dismissive attitude notwithstanding, that potential investor came through with a nine-figure investment.

BE CAREFUL BECAUSE STORIES PROPAGATE

A story rarely stops with its initial audience; instead, it takes a life of its own, traveling from listener to listener. Unbeknownst to me, toward the end of my fateful day at Lehman Brothers, my future boss took the story about my being a professional blackjack player to his boss and said, "We need to hire this guy today!" Thus, my decades-long Wall Street career was launched.

Sometimes, stories propagate in ways that are not only unpredictable but also undesirable. This is why you should be extra careful with your narrative, especially when it comes to discussing other people. A senior manager once made the mistake of speaking negatively about his current CEO while interviewing with a future one, not realizing that the two CEOs were neighbors. Not only did his interview end disastrously but he also found himself without a job shortly thereafter. The same thing happened to a young Wall Street trader who made up fanciful numbers about his job offer from a competitor. The lie was quickly discovered because the heads of the two trading desks happened to be friends.

Since connections of this nature are impossible to know ahead of time, I suggest asking yourself a simple question before saying anything during an interview: "Would I be okay with its being printed on the front page of *The New York Times*?" If the answer is anything but "yes," change your story.

IN CONCLUSION

A compelling narrative is the best way to get your point across during a negotiation. To the extent possible, stick to the truth, but don't hesitate to fabricate a narrative if necessary, especially when asked "Why are you looking for a job?" Make sure you read the room and tailor your story appropriately for the intended audience. Also make sure you don't say anything that could jeopardize your position.

CHAPTER 8

INFORMATION IS POWER

IN THE ANCIENT Chinese military treatise, *The Art of War*, Sun Tzu writes:

> *"Whether the object be to crush an army, to storm a city, or to assassinate an individual, it is always necessary to begin by finding out the names of the attendants, the aides-de-camp, and doorkeepers and sentries of the general in command."*

In other words, you need information to win a war. This principle also applies to negotiations, where the side possessing superior information usually prevails. The question then becomes: How can a lone individual overcome the immense informational disadvantage against a corporate juggernaut that employs thousands of people? For the answer, we only need to look at the next sentence of Sun Tzu's text.

"Our spies must be commissioned to ascertain these."

Sun Tzu makes it clear that information cannot be divined, nor can you rely on guesswork. The only means of acquiring critical information is via secret sources, otherwise known as spies. I have employed the same approach for the past quarter-century, but with one crucial difference. Unlike Sun Tzu, who recommends, "Pay your spies well," I don't believe in paying for information. I don't even consider my sources to be spies, but a loosely connected network of friends, acquaintances, and former clients. At no point do I expect any of them to reveal confidential information that would risk jeopardizing their own careers. The aim is not to have a source compromise their integrity but to have them divulge information that falls somewhere between the public and the confidential.

Information is a two-way street. The other side is also looking for clues that might improve their negotiating position. Hence, it is just as important not to share critical information as it is to collect it. As we shall see below, withholding crucial facts from your opponent can enhance your advantage and lead to a significantly better outcome.

ADAPT TO NEW INFORMATION

As Chapter 1 makes clear, a successful negotiation requires you to adapt to changing circumstances. Focusing on the next move, and only the next move, requires you to modify your strategy as new information comes to light. That intelligence is sometimes contained in a response delivered by the other side, and at other times, it is acquired from a source. No matter the origin, all available information must be considered while contemplating your next move.

There are times when the optimal move is a sharp U-turn, as

was the case with Kevin in Chapter 5. Likewise, in late 2004, I was compelled to abandon my policy of ignoring headhunters' calls and instead actively began seeking a new job. For the past five years, I had remained solely focused on my own performance, paying little attention to the goings-on around me. However, as soon as I became aware of the existential dangers faced by my employer, a large Swiss bank, I decided to get as far away from the company as I could. It is worth noting that I could not have discovered this information independently, as many of the bank's strategies were beyond my area of expertise. A handful of trusted Wall Street sources helped me to understand where and how the bank had gone astray. The insights from those conversations led to my decision to leave the company in 2005. Hence, I avoided significant professional and financial damage when the bank nearly collapsed in 2008. Such is the power of good information.

NO INFORMATION IS TOO SMALL

Much like Archimedes' lever, sometimes a negotiation can turn on the smallest piece of information. In Andrew's case, it was a passing comment by the lady from HR. Similarly, when I was trying to buy a house in the spring of 2006, the seller's broker let slip that despite the house being on the market for two months, they had not received a single offer. That errant disclosure allowed me to purchase the property at a 20 percent discount, an astonishing concession given the booming real estate market. Without that information, I would not have dared to negotiate as aggressively as I did. In another situation, as we shall see in the next section, the negotiation hinged on what seemed like a trivial piece of information—a date in a document.

Given the volume of information that we encounter daily, filtering the signal from the noise can feel like searching for a needle in a haystack. Thankfully, as far as negotiating employment contracts go, I have discovered that focusing on two specific items of information is sufficient to get you started: who else the company has interviewed and how well suited you are for the role.

WHO ELSE HAS THE COMPANY INTERVIEWED?

A negotiation does not occur in a vacuum; it is heavily influenced by the experiences of the two parties involved. If each candidate is either rejected by the company or declines the offer, managers get increasingly desperate to hire the next person on their list. Consequently, while negotiating with a corporation, it helps to know how the candidate search has unfolded so far. You do not need to know the identities of the candidates that came before you; a rough idea of their number will suffice. Hiring managers will disclose that information sometimes, but at other times, you will need to rely on industry sources. In my case, even before interviewing with a British hedge fund in early 2005, I knew that they had rejected no less than 15 candidates for the role. By the time the company eventually offered me the job, I knew they had run out of options. That knowledge strengthened my hand and allowed me to extract concessions that would have been otherwise impossible.

In another case, I could not ascertain how many candidates

had preceded my client. Nevertheless, the information contained in an internal company document—inexplicably forwarded by the hiring manager to my client—gave the game away. In addition to listing the job description and the required qualifications, which made my client a perfect fit for the role, the document also included the date when the company had initiated efforts to fill the position. That date meant that the search for a suitable candidate had been ongoing for two-and-a-half months, a duration considerably longer than was widely known. Moreover, given the critical nature of the role—managing the firm's Internet strategy—I figured that the company could not afford to wait any longer. Knowing this, I negotiated far more aggressively than I would have if the search had only just begun. If the manager had simply removed the date from the document, she would have been able to hire my client for considerably less.

HOW MUCH OF A FIT ARE YOU?

Knowing the history of a company's job search is not enough to maximize your advantage; you should also have a keen awareness of how well suited you are for the role. Companies will pay more for an individual who fits the role perfectly as opposed to someone who is merely adequate. It is not unusual for managers to tell candidates how perfect they are for the job. Similarly, headhunters have occasionally informed my clients that the company is not considering any other candidate because they believe that they've found the perfect one. Normally, I would discount anything a future manager or a headhunter says, but not when their statements weaken their own negotiating position. I have never come across a situation where a company has employed Jedi mind tricks to lull an individual into a false sense of comfort. What could they possibly hope to gain from such a maneuver?

As with the Internet strategy position in the previous section, it is also worth figuring out the importance of the role for the company. Are you merely a small part of a big machine, or are you a linchpin of their strategy? While no one is indispensable, it is also true that finding a replacement takes time. Given that time is indeed money in the corporate world, companies will pay more for a bird in hand that can start generating revenue quickly.

KEEP YOUR CARDS CLOSE TO YOUR VEST

In any game of partial information, it is just as important not to disclose critical information as it is to unearth it. If prospective managers were to learn that you were unhappy in your current job or were underpaid, they would offer you less money. Therefore, you should never speak negatively about your current employer in the interview. It doesn't take a genius to figure out that you might do the same about this company in future. Hence, it is best to accentuate the positive about the future employer, no matter how insincere it sounds.

Keeping your cards close to your vest is particularly important when you are leaving one company to go to the next. In virtually every such situation that I've been involved in, managers tried hard to find out where their valued employee was headed. Except for a handful of cases, I almost never allow an individual to disclose what they are getting paid or where they are going. No matter how much pressure their current bosses apply, I ask every client to stick to a simple yet effective line: *The terms of the contract prohibit me from disclosing this information.* This line works because managers know that every employment contract contains a confidentiality clause. Yet, they often fail to realize that you haven't signed the contract yet—otherwise, you wouldn't be in their office, negotiating the terms for staying.

If your bosses were to learn what you were getting offered away, they would not pay you a penny more. In the absence of that information, they are forced to figure out on their own what you are worth to them. There is a distinct possibility that their number might be higher than your current offer. This is exactly what happened in one of my earlier Wall Street negotiations, where I helped a coworker—and friend—secure a significantly higher offer from our employer. In the summer of 1999, Greg and I were both working at a mid-tier investment bank when a lower-tier competitor tried to hire him. While he was thrilled with their offer—$750,000 a year for two years—he was less than enthusiastic about joining a firm with a significantly smaller market presence. So, we decided to use the job offer to see what we could get from our employer[6].

It came as no surprise that once his bosses learned that he was contemplating leaving, they relentlessly interrogated him about where he was going and for how much. As instructed, he

---

[6] It is worth pointing out that by helping a colleague extract more money from our employer, I was violating my own terms of employment. I would be careful about this in the future, but in the summer of 1999, I was blissfully unaware of these repercussions.

provided a variety of evasive answers to their questions, one of which was the line I mentioned above. Had senior management known that the competing offer was for $750,000 a year, they would likely have capped their offer at $700,000. Leaving one job and starting another is stressful, and his bosses would reasonably have expected him to stay for less. Likewise, knowing that his offer was from a small broker-dealer would have caused them to reduce the offer even further. It is a well-known fact that smaller, less prestigious firms must pay more to recruit from their larger, more established competitors. In the absence of that knowledge, Greg's bosses assumed that he was being courted by a like-sized rival, if not larger. Managers are a paranoid lot and will tend to assume the worst if they don't know where you are going, which in turn improves your negotiating position.

It wasn't easy[7], but when the dust settled, our employer agreed to pay Greg $950,000 a year for two years to prevent him from leaving. By playing his cards close to his vest, my friend secured nearly half-a-million dollars extra. A few months later, his bosses did figure out the destination firm, but by then, it was too late. The contracts had already been signed.

Incidentally, I make an exception to this rule (about where the individual is headed) when there is corporate rivalry to be exploited, as was the case with Credit Suisse versus Goldman Sachs in Chapter 5.

The importance of playing one's cards close to the vest is equally valid in other types of negotiations as well. I was able to negotiate a lower price for my house by keeping two critical

---

[7] The story is contained in Chapter 29 of *Play It Right*.

pieces of information to myself. If the seller had known that we had seen and rejected 50 houses so far, he would have rightfully expected us to pay more for the one house we found desirable. Furthermore, we were running out of time. With only three months until the start of the school year, we needed to not only finalize the purchase but also move into the house without delay. Once again, that information would have strengthened the seller's hand. His broker, on the other hand, did him a disservice by letting me know that there were no other interested buyers for the property.

NOT ALL INFORMATION IS USABLE

In any employment-related negotiation, there is one item of information that I consider off limits: what someone else at the company gets paid. This issue is particularly important when you are trying to negotiate with your current employer. Employee compensation in any corporation is regarded as highly confidential and is not accessible to you. Your colleagues may choose to share it voluntarily, but you cannot necessarily believe them. Even if they allow you to view their pay stub, this information remains unusable. Its use would alert your managers to the fact that your coworker has breached the terms of their employment. And if you somehow manage to discover their salary without their knowledge, then you are asking to be dismissed for cause.

In the unlikely event that you get past all of these hurdles, you should still refrain from mentioning another employee's compensation. A manager can easily counter your demand by saying, "Let's say we made a mistake with that person and paid them too much. Does that mean that we must repeat the same error with you?" As you can see, there is no good answer to that question.

In addition, arguing that another individual's pay is too high also goes against my fundamental principles. My goal in any negotiation is to extract more from large corporations, not to reduce someone else's compensation. While unlikely, the company could simply lower the other person's pay to bring it more in line with yours, thereby undermining the crux of your argument.

However, you should still do your homework and figure out your market value from publicly available information. For example, salary details from a widely circulated job listing are acceptable to use during your negotiations, as is any other information that can be deemed to be public. In the financial industry, it is not unusual for contracts, especially big-ticket ones, to become common knowledge. All it takes is for one individual to leak it to someone, and the story spreads like wildfire. It is impossible to know if the numbers making the rounds are even accurate, but I have no hesitation in using them if they have the potential to help my client.

BUILDING AN INFORMATION NETWORK

Before you can put a network to use, you'll obviously need to build one. While there is no hard and fast rule about how to go about cultivating sources, the two things I can say with certainty are that it takes time and requires trust. Meaningful relationships are not developed overnight and require both parties to believe that they are being honest with each other. Moreover, sources must have faith that their identities will be jealously guarded and never be disclosed. Consequently, it is best for a professional network to remain out of view, as is the case with mine. I am willing to share any information that helps a client secure a better deal, but I never share from where I acquired it. Likewise, every client has strict instructions to never reveal my involvement in their affairs. In case you are wondering, I have taken great pains to hide the identities of my clients in this book. Other than the individuals directly involved in these negotiations, it would be very difficult for anyone else to figure out who they are.

A network, as you might expect, cannot be a one-way street. You should be just as willing to give information as you are to seek it. Otherwise, it is only a matter of time before your phone calls are ignored and your messages go unanswered. While I do not accept payment for my assistance during a negotiation, I do expect a client to share their expertise when I need it (most likely to help another client). Three decades on, I can confidently say that the glue that has held my professional network together is, in a word, negotiating.

IN CONCLUSION

It would be impossible for anyone to argue against the value of information during a negotiation. Without it, you wouldn't know how to respond to the changing circumstances as they arise. Sometimes, a negotiation can hinge on the smallest of details, so pay careful attention to all available information before deciding your next move. Conversely, make sure you reveal as little as possible about your situation, especially when it comes to the reasons why you are searching for a new job. Take the time and effort to cultivate (and maintain) reliable sources that can provide you with information when you need it.

CHAPTER 9

FOCUS ON THE GAME, NOT MONEY

IT MAY COME as a surprise to you that the caliber of negotiation does not automatically rise with the amounts in question. I have known vegetable sellers in New Delhi who were better negotiators than managers on Wall Street. That is not to say that one was a born negotiator and the other wasn't; it is simply a matter of training and practice. That's why I take on every client who comes my way and treat every case as an opportunity to improve my expertise. I do so by maintaining my focus squarely on the game and never on the amounts involved. Likewise, my sense of satisfaction with the end result is not a function of the size of the contract, but of the quality of my play. In every aspect of my professional life—from blackjack to financial markets to negotiating—I consider money to be a side effect of a game played well; it is not my primary objective. The fact that the money might go to someone else also makes no difference to me. I negotiate for others with the same zeal with which I negotiate for myself.

That, however, is easier said than done. Even if I am able to distance myself from money, the same cannot be said for my clients. While I understand that it is a human tendency to speculate about what one can do with additional dollars, it is also foolish to count your chickens before they hatch. As long as I am sitting at a blackjack table, a black chip is merely a black chip, and not a hundred-dollar bill. There will be plenty of time for counting "when the dealin's done," as Kenny Rogers so astutely observed[8].

GAMES ARE SERIOUS BUSINESS

It may appear that I am being frivolous by reducing negotiating to a game. However, there is nothing trivial about games. An entire branch of economics and mathematics—game theory—is dedicated to understanding interactions between competing counterparties and determining the optimal strategy for a favorable outcome. This definition could just as easily apply to negotiating. A wide variety of fields use game theory today, including economics, business, politics, and international relations, to understand and ultimately resolve conflicts. It can even be argued that Sun Tzu's *Art of War* provides a theoretical framework for a game with life-and-death consequences. It is no coincidence that the term "wargames" is applied to military simulations.

A game, even a single-player game, cannot be played without an opponent. Even Solitaire, the most well-known one-player

---

[8] Lyrics to *The Gambler*

game, requires you to overcome an inanimate object—a randomly shuffled deck of playing cards. Likewise, a brick wall can be your opponent when it comes to practicing tennis. While negotiating, I consider the entire corporate edifice to be my adversary because, as discussed before, it is impossible to know who the company's shot caller is. Overcoming the trifecta of management, HR, and legal hurdles is a significant challenge, and I believe it requires a methodical approach. However, before implementing any method for victory, you need to understand the rules of the game.

GAMES HAVE RULES

Perhaps the most significant rule of negotiating is that the moment you respond to any offer with a counterproposal, the company's original offer is no longer valid. As mentioned earlier, this is why there are no risk-free moves in a negotiation. No matter what action you take, it reveals information about your position, thereby allowing the other side to adjust accordingly. I have a difficult time explaining this rule to first-time clients who tend to consider any job offer as a free option to demand even more. I routinely say no to corporations, but I do so only after giving serious consideration to their latest proposals. Therefore, at every step of the process, I ask every client a straightforward question:

"If this was their best and final offer, would you take it?"

I ask this question despite having no intention of accepting the company's proposal. The client's answer, nevertheless, has a significant impact on how I play the game from there on. Each of the three possible answers—yes, no, or maybe—requires a different approach to the problem.

An information technology (IT) professional who had apparently never negotiated before had a particularly difficult time grasping this fundamental rule of negotiating. A large company had offered to pay him $240,000 for a mid-level management position, but, as is often the case, he wanted more. So, I began with my standard question.

"I am not saying that we have to accept their starting offer. However, if they had absolutely no room in this number, would you accept it?"

"Why do I need to answer that now?"

"Because it determines how we proceed."

"I don't know," he replied, which is always a frustrating answer.

"So, there is a chance that your answer could be yes," I prodded.

"Yes, but I really don't want to," he replied.

With this knowledge in hand, I suggested that he gently nudge the corporation upward by saying, "Thank you for the offer. After giving it serious consideration, I think it is a little low. I was hoping for something in the vicinity of $300,000."

I had purposefully asked him to use the words "hoping" and "vicinity" in the email to soften his request for a higher salary. I would have taken a more aggressive tack if his answer to my question had been "Absolutely not!" Incidentally, "vicinity" always means less in a negotiation, and never a penny more.

The HR representative who was tasked with communicating with my client, but almost certainly not with making any decisions, returned with, "We can't do $300,000, but we can improve to $260,000."

My client was still dissatisfied.

"I want $275,000," he said to me.

"I understand, but what if this was their final offer? Would you accept it?"

"Yes," he replied grudgingly. "I don't have any other prospects."

"In that case, I suggest you ask the guy from HR a simple question: Is this your best offer?"

"Why can't I just ask for a higher number?" my client objected.

"Because you could lose the existing offer."

"What do you mean? Why can't we ask for $275,000 and then go back and accept $260,000 if they refuse?"

My client was genuinely shocked to learn that he could not count on the latest offer still being on the table once he had countered.

"Why is that?" he asked, in all seriousness.

"By asking for more, you have disclosed that you are not happy accepting $260,000. That fact alone could force the company to reconsider their offer, especially if they had to stretch to get this far. Let's just say, for argument's sake, that you were to demand a million dollars. Knowing this, should the company still want to hire you for $260,000?"

"What stops them from simply saying 'Yes, this is our best?'"

"Nothing," I replied. "But this is the only way to ask for more without losing the offer. Also, the company is taking a risk with that answer, as you might turn them down. A yes means that they are willing to accept that possibility."

It took some effort to get the IT professional to understand this basic rule of negotiating, but he got there in the end. Not surprisingly, the company came back with, "This is our best and final number," which led to our responding with, "In that case, I am delighted to accept your offer." There is no doubt in my mind that if left to his own devices, he would have fumbled the matter.

Another negotiating rule that I abide by is to never ask for more once you've accepted an offer. While I treat every verbal agreement as the conclusion of the negotiation, it is by no means the end of the road. Your acceptance is non-binding at this stage, and there is no assurance that you will sign on the dotted line. Virtually every employment contract that I've seen contains clauses that can be used as an escape hatch, if needed. The most common of these is the company's non-compete period, but more on that later.

Moreover, even signing a contract does not commit you to joining the company. Before you do a U-turn of this nature, however, be sure to examine the document carefully to see if you will incur a penalty. By and large, employment contracts allow both sides to walk away before the employee's start date. It is not unheard of for corporations to rescind fully executed job offers, so you should not feel guilty about doing the same.

GAMES REQUIRE STRATEGY

A game cannot be played well without a method, at least not for any length of time. A blackjack player relying on gut instinct can get lucky for a few hands, but long-term success is impossible without a mathematically sound strategy. Similarly, achieving longevity in financial markets requires a robust system that provides a demonstrable edge. I feel the same way about negotiating, where repeatable success requires a rigorous method.

A method, however, is only a necessary condition, and not a sufficient one, for attaining victory. Continued success also demands practice and discipline. This is why I take every case that comes my way and why I never refuse a client, no matter how difficult they might prove to be. Even with the most intractable individuals, I end up learning something (about the negotiating process) that I didn't know before. The added knowledge allows me to improve my skill, thereby making me a better negotiator for future clients. Practice does indeed make perfect.

The goal with any game is to practice enough for your actions to become reflexive. Seasoned poker players can react instinctively to almost any game situation because of the muscle memory developed over years of play, as can most professional athletes. With decades of negotiating under my belt, I too have developed muscle memory that allows me to respond to most situations intuitively. In most cases, I find that the optimal move is fairly apparent (at least to me). And if that's not the case, I simply sit still until the correct move reveals itself. Unlike a chess match, negotiating is not bound to a clock.

The alternative to playing a game strategically is to play emotionally, which is a surefire recipe for failure. Emotions invariably cloud your thinking and cause you to make moves that are, in a word, suboptimal. Perhaps my greatest contribution to any negotiation is making sure that the client puts their emotions aside and acts rationally. I do so by reducing even the most involved negotiations to a series of small steps. I know that as long as every small move is made with cold, hard logic, the final result will take care of itself. In contrast, whenever a client has acted impulsively, the outcome has been nothing short of disastrous.

A salesperson was to discover this lesson the hard way. At the end of a long and cumbersome process, we had managed to secure an excellent deal from a competitor and even gotten his current employer to match the terms. Unfortunately, my client ignored repeated entreaties from senior management and allowed a single statement from a mid-level manager to get to him instead.

"It looks like you are not happy here, so you should leave."

Rightfully, he should have ignored the comment, especially given that the said manager's bosses had told my client the exact opposite. My client, however, saw the remark as a mark of disrespect and reacted spontaneously by walking out. Five years later, with his career now in a tailspin, he would look back and rue the day he allowed his emotions to get the better of him.

GAMES HAVE WINNERS AND LOSERS

When it comes to employment-related matters, I don't subscribe to the win-win school of negotiating. I view it as a zero-sum game, where one side's gain is the other side's loss. Consequently, much like a poker hand or a tennis match, a negotiation too has only one winner. As with any game of skill, winning or losing in this game is a direct function of a player's expertise.

In any game, you need to keep score to know who won. For lack of a better alternative, money often (but not always) serves as the means of scoring a negotiation. From my perspective, every dollar that migrates from a corporation to an individual effectively scores a point in our favor. I feel like I've won if I can help a client secure a better deal than they could have managed themselves, something that occurs far more frequently than not. However, negotiating is one game where the highest score doesn't always win. I often advise clients to accept less money from more reputed firms that offer better career prospects. The goal is not to maximize one year's pay but to focus on the long run. Moreover, a legally enforceable contract that offers a smaller amount is preferable to one that promises a larger payout but is worded ambiguously.

Furthermore, I do not consider the lack of a deal as tantamount to losing the game. Sometimes, the two sides have wildly different expectations, and there is just no way to bridge the gap. At other times, the intelligence gained during the negotiation proves more valuable than a signed contract. Nevertheless, I consider myself to have lost the game when my actions are directly responsible for a negotiation falling apart, which, thankfully, happens extremely rarely.

GAMES ARE FUN

Like most games, negotiating can be a great deal of fun. There are few things I enjoy more than being embroiled in a complicated negotiation against a corporate behemoth. That is not to say that negotiations are stress-free, but then, what high-stakes game is? It is nearly impossible to excel at any activity in life unless you also enjoy it. Negotiating, for me, is a choice borne out of enjoyment and not out of compulsion. That is not the case for many of my clients, who feel weighed down by the process. It takes a great deal of effort, but right from the start, I try to impart a sense of fun about the upcoming journey. Despite my best efforts, many cannot find any joy in the process. One of those individuals was a first-time client called Matt, who breathed a long sigh of relief at the end of the negotiation.

"Boy, am I glad that's over!"

"What do you mean?" I asked.

"That was one of the most stressful things I have ever been through," he replied.

I didn't have the heart to tell him that this was my easiest negotiation in years. I would negotiate several more times for Matt over the next decade or so, where he would see for himself what "stressful" looks like.

Some clients, on the other hand, embrace the idea of having fun during a negotiation. That makes my life easier and often leads to a better outcome too. A carefree individual makes for a better player than one who feels the weight of the world on their shoulders. Hence, to the extent possible, try and enjoy yourself while negotiating. Always remember: It's just a game.

IN CONCLUSION

The parallels between games and negotiating cannot be overstated. It makes sense, therefore, that many of the principles of game theory can also be applied to negotiations. As with any game of skill, repeatable success requires a robust strategy coupled with practice and discipline. While negotiating, never forget the fact that your next move might erase the previous offer and that success hinges upon a series of small moves made correctly. Even though negotiating is serious business, don't forget to have fun while you're doing it.

CHAPTER 10

ACT STRONG WHEN WEAK, WEAK WHEN STRONG

DECEPTION IS AN integral part of any game, more so when the two sides operate with incomplete information. To successfully mislead your opponent, you need to hide your true position and make them believe that it is something else entirely. A poker player holding a pair of aces feigns weakness to keep other players in the hand. A show of strength on their part, via a large bet, will cause their opponents to immediately fold, thereby reducing the player's profit potential. Likewise, if a player holding a two-seven-offsuit (the worst starting hand in Texas Hold'em) is to have any hope of winning the hand, they need to project strength. Remember, the best hand doesn't always win in poker. Nor does the side with the best negotiating position.

STRENGTH IS RELATIVE

In any game, strength and weakness are relative. You could be one of the fastest runners in the world, but if you are up against Usain Bolt, you will likely lose. Likewise, the lowest ranked professional golfer would easily overcome a casual player, even if the part-timer routinely beats everyone at their club. Hence, the first step in any contest is to determine how you stack up against the opposition.

This issue is of even greater importance in games like poker and negotiating, where part of the information remains hidden. The question then becomes: How do you calibrate your play without knowing the strength (or weakness) of your opponent? The answer, in a word, is perception. In the absence of information, both sides are forced to act on the basis of their perception of the other side's strength. Thus, it is vital to fake strength when you are, in fact, weak and vice versa. The former enables you to extract more from the other side, and the latter allows you to explore alternatives, as we shall see later in this chapter.

In Chapter 1, Thomas successfully projected strength—"I knew it then, and I know it now!"—when, in reality, his position was incredibly weak. In financial markets, sitting out for five years is tantamount to writing your career obituary. He would have considered himself lucky to even get a job, let alone one with a seven-figure contract. The investment bank, though, bought his act and, as a result, paid dearly for it. The company's hand was strong, but the managers unwittingly played it weak. That, to me, is the epitome of poor gamesmanship. Feigning weakness is a good idea only when it is done knowingly. Otherwise, you are deceiving yourself and not your opponent.

MISLEAD, BUT DON'T LIE

Misleading your opponent is one thing; lying is another. While I am all in favor of the former, I am strongly against the latter. My opposition to lying is not based on moral or ethical grounds—they have no place in a conflict—but on a sense of pragmatism. I have known of instances where a candidate lied during an interview, got caught, and was summarily removed from consideration. Even if you manage to make it through the hiring process without being discovered, the risk persists for as long as you work at the company and possibly even beyond. Every employment offer that I've come across contains language that voids the contract if any false representations by the individual come to light.

That's precisely what happened to a marketing specialist who, for some inexplicable reason, listed two undergraduate degrees from two far-flung universities on her résumé. Even more inexplicably, the company did not bother to verify her educational background before hiring her. The lie was discovered a few months later when the corporation got around to performing a background check on their new hire. She did get fired, but despite deserving it, she did not get terminated for cause. Moreover, the company offered her a five-figure sum as they showed her the door. Such is the power of a release.

To clarify, when I mention lies, I refer to verifiable facts, not opinions. With the former, I insist on sticking to the truth, but with the latter, embellishment is almost a requirement in any job interview.

DISCLOSE INFORMATION SELECTIVELY

There is another reason why every client of mine has strict instructions never to explicitly lie to our opponent—there is no artistry in it. The real challenge lies in creating a false impression without having to resort to falsehoods. The best way to achieve that goal is via selective disclosure of information. By carefully choosing what is said (and what is left unsaid), you allow your opponent to fill in the blanks according to their own predisposition. For instance, when you claim that you are looking for a job at a company because you want to work with the best and the brightest, you might be reinforcing what your interviewer already believes. If so, they are unlikely to dig any further into your motivations for making the move.

In another case, a client of mine found herself in a dilemma while discussing her past compensation with a future employer. Though the numbers were high enough, the trend was a problem. Her pay for the past three years had been $1.8 million, $1.5 million, and $1.2 million, respectively. If the progression were to continue, the company could expect to hire her for less than $1 million. If, on the other hand, the three numbers had been reversed, she could rightfully expect to be paid double that amount. Lying about the numbers was out of the question, nor could she refuse to answer the question on compensation for fear of raising a red flag. So, I instructed her to say the following:

"My pay for the last three years has ranged from $1.2 million to $1.8 million with an average of $1.5 million."

This statement was demonstrably true, even though it left out an important detail. It allowed her interviewers to make the logical (but incorrect) conclusion that her pay must have risen over the last three years. Although corporations in New York are no longer permitted to ask questions about an individual's past compensation, the fact remains that selective disclosure of information can mask a weak position.

There are scenarios where an individual might need to execute both of these maneuvers simultaneously: feigning weakness with one counterparty while projecting strength with another. Such was the case with the continuing story of Andrew, who, you might recall, had successfully called the company's bluff and neutralized the threat of cause. Even though he was thrilled with the outcome, I couldn't help feeling a twinge of disappointment at the final result. The game had ended too soon for me.

Fortunately, while one game had ended prematurely, another began almost immediately. There was still the matter of Andrew finding a new job. I had asked him to settle with the bank first, before exploring employment opportunities. Future managers were bound to inquire why he was no longer at his previous job, and I wanted to avoid the term "cause" being part of that conversation. Had we failed in our negotiations with his previous employer, that word would have severely weakened his negotiating position, if not destroyed his employment prospects altogether. A few companies might have been willing to look past it, but they would have offered him rock-bottom terms. With cause no longer an issue, he could look for a new position without worry.

FEIGNING WEAKNESS

Two early suitors emerged for Andrew—a hedge fund and a small broker-dealer. Given his experience over the last 12 months—his former employer was also a broker-dealer, albeit a large one—Andrew indicated a strong preference for the hedge fund. I didn't care one way or the other; all I wanted was to negotiate the best possible deal.

The hedge fund, however, had other plans and made an offer that I felt was too low. The payout percentage—in single digits—was half of what it should have been, especially because a third of his compensation was to be deferred for several years. Unfortunately, Andrew disagreed, and to my disappointment, swiftly reached an agreement with the hedge fund's owner. A verbal understanding, however, is one thing; a signed contract is an entirely different matter.

I gave in on most issues, but I put my foot down regarding one clause in the contract. The hedge fund had insisted upon a six-month non-compete, which I felt was too long. A non-compete clause imposes a waiting period between an employee leaving one job and starting another, effectively requiring them to remain unemployed during that time.

When entering into an employment agreement, most people tend to gloss over the conditions governing their departure from the firm. However, given that the average tenure of a job is only a handful of years, those clauses must be carefully examined. The longer the non-compete, the harder it becomes for an employee to leave, which is exactly what every employer wants. I have known of instances where unnoticed paragraphs sentenced ex-employees to 18 months of thumb twiddling.

In Andrew's case, I would have accepted a graduated non-compete, starting at three months and gradually increasing to six months as he got comfortable in his new role. But the hedge fund disagreed. They dug in their heels as did we, causing the negotiation to reach a stalemate.

One Friday afternoon, I was on my way home when Andrew called.

"The hedge fund wants to talk," he said.

"When?"

"In 15 minutes."

"Stall them for a bit. I'll be there in half an hour," I said and turned my car toward his house. Once there, I quickly explained my plan, which, unbeknownst to Andrew, I had executed several times with other clients.

The two of us would sit in a quiet room with a notepad and a pencil. When the hedge fund called, he was to put them on speaker phone and carry on conversing as normal. Throughout the phone call, I would scribble on the notepad to guide Andrew's responses. This was a tried and tested tactic for me. No company ever figured out that they were negotiating directly with me in real time.

Andrew and I moved into the dining room, shut all the doors, and placed a notepad between us. When his cellphone rang, we didn't answer it until the fifth ring—anything to keep the opponent on edge.

The hedge fund owner began by listing reasons why the company needed a lengthy non-compete, none of which were valid. We could have easily refuted his logic, but I asked Andrew not to push back and pretend to be wishy-washy instead. The hedge fund's offer was set to expire in two hours, and I hoped to use my client's indecisiveness to buy us more time. The conversation meandered for what seemed like ages, and in his frustration, the owner yielded ever so slightly.

"It's Friday afternoon. Why don't you think about it over the weekend and call us on Monday?"

Here it was—the opening I had been searching for. The owner didn't realize it, but he had made a major mistake—one that would cost him the game.

"HANG UP NOW," I wrote furiously.

Andrew shot me a puzzled look, but quickly ended the phone call.

"What's the matter?"

"We have what we need," I replied.

"And what's that?"

"Time."

"Huh?"

"The hedge fund offer was set to expire today. Now we have another two-and-a-half days."

"And what are we going to do with that time?" my client wondered.

"Negotiate with the broker-dealer."

Andrew's jaw hit the floor.

"What?"

This was not part of his plan. If it were up to him, he would have signed the contract that afternoon. Still, he knew that he had nothing to lose. The hedge fund job would still be there on Monday morning.

We had purposefully kept the hedge fund in the dark about

the broker-dealer being in the mix. Our hand was strong—there was another bidder for Andrew—but we had played it as if it were weak. Thus, we had allowed the hedge fund owner to believe that he was the only game in town. If he'd had any inkling about another company's interest in Andrew, he would have stood firm on the afternoon deadline, which would have forced my client to sign. The owner wasn't stupid, just overconfident. After all, he must have thought, what could possibly go wrong between Friday evening and Monday morning? As it turned out for him, everything.

FEIGNING STRENGTH

With Andrew's second suitor, the broker-dealer, our approach was the exact opposite of what we did with the hedge fund. Our hand was weak—the hedge fund's terms were abysmal—but we played it from a position of strength.

Throughout the process, even as we held him at bay, we had kept the broker-dealer firm's CEO updated about the hedge fund's interest in Andrew. It was done with the sole purpose of putting him on the defensive. The CEO knew as well as anybody that hedge funds occupied the top of the Wall Street hierarchy, while companies like his sat near the bottom. With every passing day, he grew more and more pessimistic about his chances of getting Andrew.

A phone call on Friday evening changed that—I had to twist Andrew's arm into making it— and caused the CEO to spring into action. In direct contrast to the hedge fund, this negotiation proved to be quick and painless. By Saturday evening, we had hammered out a deal that I considered to be spectacular. In his desperation, the CEO had overshot the mark, and not by a small margin. Such is the power of projecting strength.

My client, however, was unmoved. He had decided to go to the hedge fund and that was that. He told me as much on Sunday evening as we huddled together to make a final decision.

"No!"

Andrew was shocked by my response. He rightfully believed that he would have the final say. It was, after all, his life. That would have been the case usually, but not here.

I had not stood in his way when he accepted a subpar settlement from his ex-employer for one simple reason. The only thing he had left on the table was money. Once the threat of cause had been removed, there was nothing else at risk. On that Sunday night, though, a lot more than just money was at stake, not the least of which was his future. To me, his decision appeared to be an emotional one, the result of having gotten burned by a large broker-dealer. I, on the other hand, felt that his recent experience was an outlier and unlikely to be repeated. Moreover, I felt that his skill set was better suited for the broker-dealer job. The hedge fund position, in contrast, would be a gamble for someone who had never managed money before.

Consequently, for the first time ever, I insisted that a client go against his own wishes and do as I say. The two offers were miles apart, and I could not allow him to choose the inferior one.

It took some doing, but I prevailed.

On Monday morning, Andrew told the hedge fund that he had accepted another offer. The owner was shocked, but given his stance from two days ago, he couldn't bring himself to reduce the non-compete period. Not that it would have mattered. If he'd had a sudden change of heart on the non-compete, I would have found some other reason to walk away.

Andrew thrived in his new job and never regretted turning the hedge fund down. A decade later, he is still at the broker-dealer, now one of its most valued employees.

This case is an excellent example of how a well-executed negotiation can dramatically alter one's fortunes. Reading the bank's cards correctly allowed us to call the company's bluff and get rid of the threat of cause. By pretending to be weak when we were strong, we managed to gain time from the hedge fund. By pretending to be strong when we were weak, we got the broker-dealer firm's CEO to concede too much. Had any one of those moves been made incorrectly, my client would have been significantly worse off.

IN CONCLUSION

A game of imperfect information necessitates misleading your opponent about the relative strength of your position. Nevertheless, I am against lying to accomplish that goal; I prefer to rely on selective disclosure of information instead. Your choice to portray strength or weakness should be based on what you aim to gain from the other side, rather than on your actual position. In negotiation, as in poker, you don't play the cards in front of you; you play the person across from you. Maybe, just maybe, they have a hand that's worse than yours.

CHAPTER 11

BE ANGRY ONLY WHEN YOU ARE CALM

"If you can keep your head when all about you
Are losing theirs and blaming it on you"
— *If* by Rudyard Kipling

ANYONE WHO FINDS themselves in a difficult situation would benefit from following Kipling's advice to his son: Avoid getting swept up in others' emotional reactions, and stay in control of your own responses. This was a lesson I learned the hard way. Without a doubt, the most difficult aspect of becoming a professional gambler was gaining control over my emotions. It was also the most rewarding. By ensuring that every move was made rationally and with unflinching logic, I gained a significant advantage in the game. Likewise, the ability to maintain my composure in tough situations has proven immensely valuable throughout my Wall Street career as well as during every negotiation. While that does not guarantee victory, it increases the probability of success.

Letting emotions dictate your play, on the other hand, is a surefire recipe for disaster. Emotions expose your vulnerabilities and cloud your thought process, placing you at a considerable disadvantage. When one feels fear, the tendency is to settle for too little. And when the opposite is true, the inclination is to go for broke. Perhaps this is why my clients find it invaluable to have an advisor by their side. It is not easy to remove oneself from one's circumstances and examine the situation with a clear and unbiased viewpoint.

A display of emotion is warranted under only two conditions. First, there must be a purpose behind the exhibition, perhaps as simple as throwing the other side off-balance. Much like a gambler on tilt, an unbalanced adversary is prone to making errors. Second and far more important, you must be calm on the inside even as you portray the exact opposite on the outside. Only then will you be able to pick up clues in your opponent's reactions and plot the best way forward.

Nowhere is this truer than when dealing with the most powerful of human emotions. Anger is a natural consequence of any conflict and is, therefore, unavoidable in a negotiation. I myself am frequently angry (mostly at corporations), but I make sure never to act out of anger. That is not to say that I deny my feelings; if anything, I do the opposite. However, instead of allowing my resentment to control me, I use it to figure out my next move. I never react in haste; I wait until I have examined the situation with a cool head. Anger that is conveyed calmly has far greater impact than an outburst in the throes of emotion. The former forces the other side to take you seriously, whereas the latter might cause them to dismiss you as hysterical. Thomas's deliberate denouncement of the investment bank's attempts to prorate his compensation was directly responsible for the corporation coming back to him, willing to negotiate. Similarly, Andrew delivered the angriest of responses in the calmest of fashions: by simply refusing to respond to the company's "final" offer.

Anger, however, is a two-way street. You will encounter anger during a negotiation too. Hence, it is critical for you to discern whether your opponent's outburst is genuine or an act designed to elicit a certain response from you. In the former case, it may be necessary to retreat to salvage the deal, while in the latter, you can ignore the spectacle and charge forward.

CONFRONTING FAKE ANGER

I would argue that anger displayed on behalf of a corporation is, more often than not, fake. Managers may be a lot of things, but they are not stupid. They know that an angry outburst is unlikely to endear them to the target of that resentment. So, why do they do it? There can be only one explanation: to get you to capitulate and accept their terms.

I first learned that lesson decades ago while negotiating with a small financial institution. We were getting close to a deal when I asked my future boss for a slight increase in my second year's compensation. His reaction—unbridled rage—took my breath away and led to my quickly agreeing to his latest proposal. As soon as I said yes, though, the manager underwent a Houdini-like metamorphosis, transforming from an angry lion to a gentle lamb. In that instant, I knew that I'd been had. The manager had put on a great act, and I had fallen for it.

That lesson came in handy a few years later when I was helping one of my long-time clients, Kevin, negotiate with a UK-based investment bank. The British, as they have done throughout history, took a divide-and-conquer approach with the five candidates under consideration for the role. The two co-heads of the business were careful to reveal only part of the information to each of the five individuals. However, since I was advising four of the five candidates, the company's cards were laid bare in front of me. This fact was unknown not only to the bank but also to each of the four individuals, one of whom was Kevin. I don't see a conflict of interest in working with multiple individuals simultaneously as they vie for the same position. I know that sooner or later, the company will have to pick a winner. If that happens to be one of my clients, then I would be better prepared for the negotiation to follow.

That's what happened here as well. It didn't take long for me to figure out who the co-heads had settled on.

I called Kevin, "You're it!"

"How do you know?"

"Never mind that," I replied, "I just do. The bank wants you, and that too in a hurry."

"Really?"

"Yes, and we are going to take them for everything," I said, which was music to my client's ears.

And take them for everything we did, to the tune of $4.5 million.

It wasn't easy, though. It never is. There is always a fight.

The co-heads, as expected, made Kevin an opening offer,

which he immediately turned down, as we had planned. A few back-and-forth discussions later, the bosses implied that they had stretched the number as far as they could.

Kevin still said no.

What happened next made me laugh, though it left my client shaken. One of the two bosses called Kevin and laid into him for not accepting their latest offer. His ranting and raving might have worked if I hadn't been involved in the matter.

"Dude, the bank is very angry with me," Kevin said.

"Don't be silly," I replied.

"The guy just yelled at me for 15 minutes straight."

"And what about the other co-head?" I asked.

"He is surprisingly calm."

To me, this seemed like classic good-cop, bad-cop strategy, where one acts in a hostile manner while the other extends an olive branch.

"Don't fall for it. Stand firm on your number."

"Okay," he replied.

Kevin has a conflict-averse personality, and it wasn't easy for him to withstand the onslaught. Conflict is often unavoidable in a negotiation, and those who shy away from it usually end up on the losing side. Moreover, in this case, I was convinced the co-head's anger signified desperation, which further strengthened my resolve not to give in. A few more heated conversations ensued, which Kevin handled the best he could without yielding, before the bosses finally capitulated and handed him an extraordinary payday. Their anger, all along, had been make-believe.

In my experience, the younger the individual, the more

likely managers are to pressure them, which annoys me no end. The fight between a company and an individual is not fair to begin with, yet managers persist in targeting the weakest. That's what a 40-year old CEO of a healthcare startup tried to do with a young woman who was barely two years out of school. Instead of simply allowing her to leave the firm and pursue other opportunities, the CEO berated her for "only thinking of herself and not the company." He demanded that she continue at her job for another six months despite the fact that her contract only required a month's notice. She almost gave in, fearing that the well-connected CEO would ruin her future employment possibilities.

"Why would he do that?" I asked.

"He is angry that I am leaving. It's not a good look for a startup to lose employees. That's why he wants me to stick around for six more months."

"Sure," I said, "but I think it looks even worse for a CEO to bad-mouth a former employee. Anyway, you cannot let your life be controlled by someone else's emotions."

"What should I do?"

"Send him an email saying that your last day will be three weeks from today, as mandated by your employment agreement. That will make it official. Whatever he says after that is moot."

She did as I asked. The CEO never spoke to her again, but more importantly, did not express any further resistance to her leaving. Nor did he trash-talk her behind her back, as she had feared.

These three examples of fake anger have one common theme: The company wanted something from the individual. My future boss wanted me to accept a lower amount, as did the co-heads with Kevin. Likewise, the startup CEO wanted his employee to stick around for longer than she was legally required to. Thus, if you confront anger that is coupled with a demand, it is likely that the emotion is not real.

Although it's not a frequent occurrence, there are times when the anger is genuine, and dealing with it requires a different approach.

CONFRONTING REAL ANGER

A genuinely angry counterparty doesn't want anything from you. Most likely, they are letting you know that your latest demand was unreasonable and that they have no interest in pursuing the matter further. At this point, whether the anger is justified or not no longer matters. There is also nothing to be gained by wondering whether you or external circumstances were responsible for their anger. You have lost whatever leverage you had, and the only thing left to do is to ask yourself: What do I want from this situation?

In Chapter 2, my client wanted nothing further from the West Coast money manager who had screamed at her, "This is not how you are supposed to negotiate." So, she simply hung up the phone and moved on with her life. Reacting to his anger and retaliating would have been a terrible idea. A conflict should only be escalated in the interest of an eventual resolution, and not just to vent your frustrations. The manager appeared to have missed this crucial point; otherwise, he wouldn't have acted as he did.

If, on the other hand, you wish to salvage the situation, then you have no other option but to retreat from your previous position. An apology similar to the one Kevin made in Chapter 5 is a possible course of action. On a few occasions, I have used intermediaries to revive dying negotiations and, at times, even acted as one. The game is essentially lost, so I'm open to trying anything that might bring the irate counterparty back to the negotiating table. There is no guarantee that these efforts will succeed, so it's best to not let matters get this far in the first place. This is why, at every step of the process, I ask the client, "If this were their final offer, would you accept it?" If the answer is yes, I proceed cautiously, making sure not to anger the other side. Even when the answer is a firm no, I still avoid charging blindly ahead and making unreasonable demands. I am not afraid of conflict, but I prefer to delay it as long as possible, if not avoid it altogether. As Sun Tzu said, "The greatest victory is that which requires no battle."

DISPLAYING ANGER

Anger is a vital tool in a negotiator's arsenal and one that many people are afraid to use. As discussed earlier, any display of anger on your part should have a clear purpose, and anger should be expressed only when you are calm. Otherwise, you might be seen as overly emotional and someone who cannot be reasoned with, which makes you an unreliable counterparty. That is not to say that hysteria doesn't have its uses. It does, but only in rare cases, as we shall see in the next section.

Decades ago, my attorney, Ted, was deeply disappointed at the contract sent by a corporation's lawyer.

"Kamal, this draft bears no resemblance to what we had agreed to. This leaves you with two options. You can either tell the company that they must have sent the wrong contract and ask them for the correct one."

"Or?"

"Or, you can tell them to f*** off." Ted said, using decidedly unlawyerly language.

I chose the latter option, although not in those words. I called the CEO and told him calmly that I did not appreciate his pulling a fast one, so I was pulling out of the negotiation. That induced a small panic, causing him to blurt out, "It's just a trivial drafting error. We can fix it."

This is typical of most corporations. Like small children, they will try to get away with anything they can, but when confronted, they will often agree to "fix it." Even though the CEO's claim of a "trivial drafting error" was laughable, I didn't challenge him on it. My goal was to get the company to fix the contract, and "fix it" they did.

In another instance, I was appalled by an escape clause that a hedge fund's lawyers had inserted into my contract.

"Let me get this straight," I asked the lead attorney, "If I lose even one penny on the first day of my employment, that allows your firm to walk away from all of its obligations outlined in this 25-page contract?"

"Why would we do that?" she replied, which was hardly an answer.

"The question is not why, but legally speaking, can you do it?" I persisted.

She hemmed and hawed for a few minutes before conceding that was indeed the case. I exclaimed, "I can't believe you would try to pull something like that!" and slammed the phone down. That display of anger was enough to get this company to also "fix it."

Sometimes, a calculated display of anger can get you out of a tough spot, as was the case when I found myself embroiled in an age-discrimination lawsuit filed by a salesman against an investment bank. The salesman had covered me for a year before I asked that someone else be assigned to me. This is a fairly common occurrence on Wall Street, where salespeople are routinely shuffled between clients. In this case, however, the investment bank used my request as an excuse to dismiss the salesman, which, in turn, led him to sue the company. Out of nowhere, I was caught between two sets of lawyers.

The bank's lawyers wanted me to testify to the salesperson's incompetence, and the salesman's lawyers wanted me to do the opposite. I, on the other hand, wanted nothing to do with it because I felt that both sides were wrong. The salesman should have toned down his partying, and the corporation should not have involved me at all. Regardless, what was done was done. The question now was: How could I get myself out of this mess without having to testify in court?

I waited until I was completely calm. Then, I let both sets of lawyers have it, separately of course.

"I don't want to be involved," I said, in the loudest voice I could muster.

"Can you please tell us what you would say on the stand?" the lawyers pleaded.

"No!" I shouted to both sides, "I refuse to discuss this with you. The only way you'll find out what I have to say is by putting me on the stand!"

This display of hostility had been designed to make each side believe that I might be sympathetic to the other. I was also betting that neither lawyer would risk calling an openly hostile witness to testify for them. A conflict is easier to resolve when both sides feel vulnerable.

The gambit paid off. I heard shortly thereafter that a settlement had been reached. I never heard from either lawyer again.

WHEN ALL ELSE FAILS, ACT CRAZY

When dealing with a large company, I avoid a hysterical display at all costs. However, sometimes, there is no other way out of a difficult situation. Such situations arise only when you are departing from a company and never the other way around. No one wants to hire an employee who is prone to emotional outbursts.

It is important to stress that no matter how unhinged your performance, it must still be an act. Furthermore, it should be designed to achieve a specific outcome, and not just to get things off your chest. The corporation's representatives must be made to believe that you are not entirely in control of your actions and that you are liable to act irrationally, which could harm both you and the company. This tactic of mutually assured damage is most effective when you are aware of a chink in the company's armor, which is typically not a difficult task since most corporations' armors are full of holes.

One such situation involved a lawyer withdrawing representation from one of my clients who had recently been fired by her employer. The lawyer had been retained by my client's ex-employer for an unrelated lawsuit. Since my client was no longer employed by the company, the lawyer wanted to end their relationship as well. However, in the absence of her consent, the withdrawal of representation needed to be approved by the court. With a hearing several weeks away, we asked the attorney a simple question.

"I understand you'd like to withdraw, but at this moment, are you still my attorney?"

To our great surprise, he refused to give us a straight answer, which made me think that maybe we were on to something. So, we asked him again, a little more firmly this time.

"Why can't you answer the simple question of whether you are my lawyer currently or not?"

Once again, there was silence. I took that as a cue to continue pestering him, making sure to ratchet up the pressure with each message:

"Is it normal for attorneys to not tell clients whether they are representing them or not?"

"Why don't you answer? A simple yes or no would suffice."

"If I don't receive a reply from you, then I'll assume you are still my attorney."

"You haven't responded, so you must still be my attorney."

"Given that you are still my attorney, I have a few questions…"

The last email did provoke a response from him. In a carefully worded reply, he answered my client's questions without admitting or denying that he was, in fact, her attorney. It was a truly astonishing example of evasion.

Throughout this exchange, my client had retained the services of another attorney, but we deliberately kept that fact concealed. We wanted to make the company-hired lawyer, and by extension her ex-employer, believe that she was so unstable that she would represent herself in court. I was betting that our two adversaries, her ex-employer and their attorney, wouldn't be willing to take that risk. Who knows what she might have said in front of the judge? As noted earlier, most corporations have skeletons in their closets that they cannot afford to have exposed.

We can't know for certain what chain of events our actions triggered. However, shortly thereafter, all her legal troubles vanished. The lawsuit was settled, thereby rendering the question of "Are you my attorney?" moot.

IN CONCLUSION

Given that the two sides have opposing objectives, conflict is an unavoidable consequence of negotiation, and anger is its natural byproduct. Therefore, a negotiator must learn to manage not only their own anger but also that of the opponent. A prospective manager's anger is likely make-believe if it is coupled with a demand that you accept their proposal. Otherwise, the emotion is likely genuine, and you should reevaluate your goals for the negotiation.

You should never express your anger unless there is a purpose behind the exhibition. You should also wait until you have calmed down inside before displaying the exact opposite outside. Otherwise, you would have wasted a perfectly good emotion.

CHAPTER 12

HAVE COURAGE

YOU SHOULD NOT be afraid of large corporations. Although they may appear intimidating from a distance, it can be a very different story up close. Even the mightiest of corporations relies upon people such as managers, HR representatives, and lawyers to do its bidding. Each of these individuals has weak points that are often laid bare during an intense negotiation and, therefore, can be exploited.

The question then arises: Why does a company bother with an individual who attempts to negotiate? The answer lies in the sole reason for a corporation's existence—to make a profit—though no company would be caught dead admitting this basic fact. Instead, virtually every corporate website stresses such words as *client service*, *partnership*, *excellence*, and my personal favorite, *integrity*. These lofty claims merely sugarcoat a corporation's raison d'être: money. Consequently, the sole reason for hiring anyone is because the corporation expects the individual to contribute to their bottom line. Even cost centers, such as HR and legal, serve the profit purpose by protecting the edifice from employees and lawsuits. The greater the profit potential a corporation sees in an individual, the more they are willing to negotiate with them. This is why you should not be fearful while negotiating: The company is not hiring you out of charity. In every corporation, a significant disparity exists between the revenue generated by an employee and their compensation. A well-executed negotiation goes a long way in shrinking that gap.

While there is no doubt that negotiating a favorable contract requires courage, it is far from the only job-related situation that demands it. It would be impossible to predict the scenarios that might require you to stand up for yourself at work. However, they all share a common theme: The company, in one way or another, is attempting to intimidate you into submission.

COURAGE WHEN FACING A BULLY

Not all acts of courage have to do with dollars and cents. Sometimes, they involve standing up to a bully. Over the years, I have seen managers behaving atrociously as they try to coerce employees into doing something that is not in the individual's interest. I consider the entire corporate complex to be the bully in these scenarios, and not simply the manager doing its bidding. For all you know, the manager's supervisors could be bullying them. The famous Tony Soprano line describing the mafia— "This thing's a pyramid. Shit runs downhill, money goes up. It's that simple."— could just as easily be applied to a corporate organizational chart. The vast majority of my clients reside at the bottom of that pyramid and, therefore, are routinely subjected to "shit" from above.

In one instance, a trading manager asked a friend of mine to *mismark* securities, which is just a fancy word for committing fraud. Knowingly placing the incorrect price on a financial instrument, if discovered, can lead to civil and criminal charges, something this manager seemed unconcerned about. My friend, on the other hand, was horrified by the request.

"That's not the right price," he protested.

"Nobody here marks their bonds correctly, so why should we?" the manager replied.

In effect, this manager was implying that the financial institution was filled with wrongdoing and they should do the same. My friend, however, had no desire to be part of a criminal enterprise and left the company shortly thereafter.

Sometimes, that's precisely what a company wants: that their employee voluntarily leave the corporate entity and join a different one. The new setup almost always leaves the employee worse off, which is the point of the exercise. The two examples of this phenomenon discussed below appear to be opposites—one concerns a spinoff and the other an acquisition— but they are identical in the bullying tactics used by the companies involved.

In the first case, a large organization wanted to transfer several employees to a small startup that it was spinning off. The company's lawyers made an informal yet insidious request of the administrative staff, two of whom were my clients.

"Please resign from your current job and accept a new position at the startup."

The duo was rightfully alarmed by this development and asked me for advice. After examining the situation, I concluded that joining the startup was too risky. So, I recommended that they turn the lawyer down. They did so, which brought out the company's true colors. In an instant, the company's enforcer went from being polite to being a bully.

"If you don't do as we ask, you will get fired and there will be no job for you at the new company," the lawyer warned the pair.

Like most people, my clients could not afford to lose their jobs, which is what the company was counting on. Nevertheless, this situation required them to be brave and to stand up for themselves, especially because I was convinced that the lawyer was bluffing.

"I am not buying it," I said. "If they really wanted to get rid of you, they would have done it by now."

"So, what should we do?"

"Tell them to go ahead and fire you if they must," I said.

"Really?"

"Yes."

I had not suggested this course of action out of a false sense of bravado. For starters, I was convinced that the threat wasn't real, else the lawyer wouldn't have made it. Corporations don't go around threatening to fire people—they just do it. Even if I happened to be wrong on this key point and their employment was terminated, the company would be required to pay them severance. Furthermore, I had no doubt that the startup job would still be there if they wanted it. All in all, I felt that there was very little downside to calling the company's bluff.

It went against all their instincts, but the pair decided to put up a fight. They informed the lawyer that they were neither resigning nor accepting the new jobs and the company was free to do whatever it wanted. They stood up to the bully, and as bullies often do, this one also backed down. The company not only did not fire my clients, but, in an astonishing turn of events, also made them co-CEOs of one of its divisions two years later.

The second situation where a company tried to pull a similar maneuver involved a larger entity acquiring a smaller one. My client was, once again, Andrew, who had become a highly valued employee of the small broker-dealer firm that I had forced him to join. A few years later, his bosses decided to sell their company to another significantly larger corporation. As expected, the lawyers placed two documents in front of him, a resignation from the old company and a job offer from the new one. Luckily, I had already warned my client not to sign any papers related to the acquisition. So, he didn't say yes, and he didn't say no; he simply ignored the lawyer's request.

In the flurry of activity leading up to the merger, Andrew's paperwork somehow slipped through the cracks. However, a week before the deal was supposed to close, all hell broke loose. Both companies realized that the linchpin of the transaction had not yet signed on the dotted line(s), thereby putting the entire deal at risk. So, his current employer did what companies do when they want something from an employee: They resorted to bullying.

"If you don't sign, we will consider you as having resigned from the old company, and that will mean forfeiting all of your deferred compensation."

I was incensed when I heard this. The company was not only trying to bully my client; it was also trying to blackmail him by using his past earnings against him. This smacked of desperation because the company's position made no sense otherwise. How could a refusal to resign be considered the same as resigning? Also, under normal circumstances, I would expect a merger to immediately vest an employee's deferred pay. It was being used as bait instead, which offended me greatly. Notwithstanding my feelings, I was convinced that the best move under the circumstances was for my client to stick to his guns and continue refusing to sign.

As with any negotiation, there was a clear purpose behind this move. Unlike the case with the spinoff above, the question here wasn't whether my client would accept the new job. He was, in fact, happy to do so. The only issue was the terms of joining. My goal was to have the company vest his deferred compensation immediately and provide him with a guaranteed pay for the next year. But before we could ask for any of those things, we had to frustrate our opponents until they asked, "What would you like in return for signing these documents?"

Unfortunately, that's not what happened. What did happen is that the acquiring company asked Andrew to visit their headquarters, over a thousand miles away. He spent the following day at the company's premises and called me as he was boarding his return flight.

"I don't get it," he said. "No one even mentioned my contract."

"Just wait," I replied, "They are playing their cards close to their vest. But time is running out, and they will have to reveal them sooner rather than later."

And reveal their cards they did, while he was mid-flight, by leaving a voicemail on his cellphone.

"Call them back and listen to their proposal. Then say that

you are getting your bags from the carousel and that you'll call them right back," I said.

He had only taken a carry-on for the day trip, but this ruse would allow us to confer before he responded. He called me shortly thereafter to tell me about the company's proposal. It took me all of 30 seconds to come up with a response.

"Tell them that this won't work."

I did the same with the company's second, third, and fourth offer. By now, hours had gone by, and my client was at home, getting antsy. If it were up to him, he would have said yes to the third offer, let alone the fourth. Instead, we forced the company to offer a fifth proposal that very evening, one that accomplished most of our objectives.

"This is outstanding!" I exclaimed.

"I know! I can't believe it." My client was ecstatic.

"Call them back and accept the offer, but make sure you do it with a sense of resignation."

As we shall see in a later chapter, you can never declare victory at the end of a negotiation. In this case, Andrew had scored a significant win, though nobody would have guessed that from his demeanor. The company asked for some minor concessions in return, which we were only too happy to accommodate. When the dust had settled, my client reflected on how matters had unfolded over the past few weeks.

"I must say that I didn't agree with all of your moves as we were making them. Looking back, though, I understand why you did what you did."

That statement, in a nutshell, captures why I help others negotiate.

COURAGE TO DO THE RIGHT THING

Even in the absence of bullying, corporations often place employees at a crossroads, forcing them to make a choice. Invariably, that choice is a decision between right and wrong, where choosing to do the right thing is usually more difficult. It is easier to go with the flow even if it is taking everyone in the wrong direction. That is why no senior Wall Street executive saw the 2008 financial crisis approaching. The CEO of Citigroup, Chuck Prince, famously said, "When the music stops ... things will be complicated. But as long as the music is playing, you've got to get up and dance. We're still dancing." The fact that he made this statement in July 2007, just before the onset of the crisis, implies that the head of one of the world's largest financial institutions was wholly unaware that he was dancing on the deck of the Titanic. And he wasn't the only one. Some variation of this groupthink had permeated the entire financial industry.

Naysayers in corporate America are either ignored or punished, which makes it extraordinarily difficult for individuals to go against the flow and challenge the prevailing orthodoxy. Nevertheless, there are times when speaking up becomes not only a moral imperative but also a strategic one, because it just might save your job. That's what happened with my friend Neil during the 2008 financial crisis.

You will recall from Chapter 7 that a large and prominent hedge fund had hired Neil as a portfolio manager even though he had never managed money. However, shortly thereafter, it became apparent that Neil was not a good fit for the role he had been hired for. Hedge fund managers tend to be brash and aggressive—everything that he wasn't. But Neil's personality was a perfect fit for another vital role at the firm: risk management. Normally, a portfolio manager transitioning to managing risk would be considered a downgrade, but not in this case. Risk managers are required to be thoughtful and deliberate—everything that he was.

In 2007, Neil shared his concerns with me about a particular strategy deployed by the hedge fund. After some deliberation, I told him that the products involved were highly risky and that I wouldn't touch them with a 10-foot pole. Over the next few months, as was his nature, he carefully pondered the matter before arriving at the same conclusion. Once he was convinced, he asked the hedge fund's owner to exit the strategy and get rid of the portfolio managers.

It was an act of extraordinary courage. Not only had the strategy been consistently profitable until then, but the portfolio managers that my friend wanted terminated had also been hand-picked by the owner himself. By taking this step, Neil was effectively questioning his boss's judgment, which is hardly ever a good idea. The owner, unsurprisingly, turned him down, saying that he saw no cause for concern. For him, the music was still playing, and the iceberg was nowhere to be seen.

The hedge fund slammed into the iceberg soon after. The following year, in 2008, the strategy resulted in losses amounting to hundreds of millions of dollars and nearly led to the collapse of the company. Irate investors blamed the firm's risk management and asked for my friend's head. In a rare display of honor, the hedge fund's owner quickly put an end to that.

"Neil came to me a year ago and asked me to get out of this

business, but I overruled him. So, if you have an issue with anyone, it is with me, not my risk manager."

Neil continued with the firm for another 15 years, ultimately advancing to the role of Chief Risk Officer before retiring from the industry. There is no doubt that a single courageous act was crucial in enabling the rest of his career.

COURAGE TO WALK AWAY

It is not always possible to fight a company from the inside and win. Corporations go to great lengths to protect themselves and their own. I saw this when I tried to effect change at an investment bank and found myself fired instead. It became clear to me that most managers would choose loyalty over competence in an underling. Therefore, it is often better to walk away from a bad situation than engage in a confrontation. I don't shy away from conflict, but I see little point in fighting a battle that I know I can't win.

My departure from the Swiss bank in 2005 was a direct outcome of this belief. I knew that trying to change the culture of a hundred-billion-dollar corporation would be an exercise in futility; nor would blowing the whistle help because nobody was listening. The only course of action open to me was to make a quiet exit. Still, I agonized over the decision for months because, for the first time in my life, I had found happiness at work. If I were wrong in my conclusions about the bank's future, I would have left the only job that I had ever loved. For all I knew, even greater dangers lurked at other companies. By quitting, I risked jumping from the frying pan into the fire. Moreover, I knew that my decision to leave one of the world's most prestigious financial institutions for an unknown hedge fund would be met with near-universal disapproval. Despite all of these concerns, I finally chose to make the move.

No one, not even I, could have predicted the reversal of fortunes that the two companies would experience over the next few years. The largest of Swiss banks nearly collapsed in 2008, whereas the unknown hedge fund grew to become the largest in Europe. My refusal to be associated with wrongdoing at the Swiss bank was the sole reason why I emerged unscathed from the great financial crisis of 2008.

Unfortunately, I have known several people who were unable to walk away from a bad situation and ended up paying dearly for it. Unlike my friend who chose to leave his job when asked to mismark securities, many others continued working at companies that engaged in similar practices. One of those individuals expressed deep regret after finding himself on the wrong side of an SEC investigation.

"I knew it was wrong. I should have walked away."

"Why didn't you?" I asked.

"I got too comfortable," he replied, as he reflected on the decision that led to his pleading guilty in a court of law.

This is why it is important to walk away while you still can.

COURAGE TO SAY NO

One of the hardest things to do in any organization is saying no to your bosses, especially when there is nothing improper about their request. The question then becomes: Why would you say no to a reasonable request from the company? For the answer, we need to examine the relationship between an employer and an employee. The employer only wants one thing from an employee: more revenue that leads to higher profits. For the employee, however, the equation is more complicated. In addition to giving you a regular paycheck, a job can also help in fulfilling other personal and professional goals. For instance, my primary objective during my Wall Street years was to play the game to the best of my ability. Consequently, all of my efforts were geared toward keeping the game going for as long as possible. My bosses, however, had very different ideas about what they wanted from me.

For two decades, every one of my hedge fund bosses tried to get me to take more risk. One of them went so far as to suggest that I add a zero to all my trades, implying that I should increase my risk-taking by a factor of 10. Given that hedge funds are in the business of taking risk, the request was entirely proper. Nevertheless, for 20 years straight, I refused to comply. My reason for doing so was straightforward: The only thing these bosses could offer as incentive was more money. I, however, had no desire to even double my compensation, let alone add another zero to it. So, I continued playing the game on my own terms for as long as I felt like playing it.

Likewise, a friend of mine once declined a promotion, much to the dismay of his bosses. The added responsibility would have elevated his standing both within and outside the company. But he was more concerned about the additional liability of managing businesses he didn't fully understand than the increased prestige of a fancy title. He said no to his bosses knowing full well that his actions would limit his career prospects from that point onward. However, not everybody wishes to scale the corporate ladder.

There is nothing wrong with seeking more money or greater visibility if that's what you want. At the same time, an employee's goals don't necessarily align with an employer's, and what is good for the corporation may not always be in the individual's best interests. If my increased risk-taking had resulted in a significant loss, I would have found myself all alone, abandoned by the very bosses who had urged me to take more risk. The same would be true for my friend if something were to go wrong with his newly acquired businesses.

IN CONCLUSION

It is impossible to navigate a professional career without coming up against situations that require you to stand up for yourself. Corporations often ask employees to take actions that are not in the individual's best interests. If the request is improper, then it's best to walk away from the company. Even if there is nothing inappropriate about the demand, before complying, you must consider whether it furthers your personal objectives. Never forget that no matter what your bosses say today, you will find yourself all alone if things go wrong in future.

CHAPTER 13

TALK THE TALK EVEN IF YOU CAN'T WALK THE WALK

A CORPORATION HAS limited time to determine a candidate's suitability, usually no more than a handful of hours. Once the individual has cleared the basic requirements for the job (education and experience, for example), the decision often comes down to intangibles such as attitude, demeanor, and how quick the person is on their feet. This is why I spend a great deal of time with every client at the start of the process, to make sure that they can talk the talk—first impressions go a long way toward turning perceptions into reality. As far as walking the walk goes, it is for the corporation to decide whether the person can do the job. The best hand doesn't always win at poker, and the most capable candidate doesn't always land the job.

BE A PICTURE OF CONFIDENCE

Perhaps the most desirable quality corporations seek in a candidate is confidence. To the naked eye, confidence and competence often appear indistinguishable from each other. A lack of confidence, therefore, creates the impression that the candidate might not know what they are talking about, which will hurt their job prospects. A job interview is essentially an exercise in selling yourself, and the better salesperson invariably wins.

The best way I know to project confidence during an interview is to provide short, crisp answers. A long-winded narrative will only make the other side suspicious. Also, providing any more detail than is necessary can open you up to new lines of attack from your interrogator. Provide them with as few openings as possible by keeping your responses concise, without unnecessary elaboration or ambiguity.

Three decades ago, my Wall Street career was launched during a single day's worth of interviews. The managers at Lehman Brothers seemed untroubled that I did not know the first thing about finance. They appeared to be more focused on my attitude and how I fielded their questions.

"Why do you want to work on Wall Street?"

"Because it's the largest casino in the world," I replied, quoting a line from a magazine. In reality, I knew nothing about how the financial industry operated. Still, my answer provided my interviewer with a clear connection between my past life and my future aspirations.

"What makes you think that you'll be successful here?"

"I haven't failed at anything yet," I said, which was a stretch. I had failed plenty of times in the past, most notably as a computer scientist. However, it was impossible for the Lehman bosses to know that.

"How do we know you'll accept the job if we offer it to you?"

"What am I doing here otherwise?" I replied, without skipping a beat.

This too was misleading. I had no desire to work on Wall Street and had flown to New York only to prove something to myself: Could a professional gambler who knew nothing about finance get hired on Wall Street?

"Are you talking to any of our competitors?"

"I have spoken to Merrill Lynch and Bear Stearns."

Technically speaking, that was the truth. I had had one conversation each with both investment banks. However, I purposefully did not mention that Merrill Lynch had rejected me the day before and Bear Stearns had yet to call me back. Fortunately, the Lehman managers did not probe any further and assumed that I was close to attaining another Wall Street job.

It went on like this for hour after hour. Despite being filled with doubt, I made sure that I was a picture of confidence. At the end of that grueling day, I had successfully talked my way into a Wall Street job.

Projecting confidence, however, does not mean that you need to have all the answers. When confronted with a question to which you do not have the answer, it is better to say, "I need to think about it some more," than to provide an evasive or incomplete response. And if you are going to discuss a topic in depth, make sure that you know more about it than the person questioning you. During my interview at Lehman, I provided expansive answers on anything to do with gambling while swatting away any business-related question with a simple "I don't know."

SPEAK THE INTERVIEWER'S LANGUAGE

Every industry has its own language. That language not only facilitates communication between professionals in that field, but it also serves as a barrier to entry for outsiders. This applies to specific roles within an industry and to individual companies. To project confidence during an interview, you'll need to familiarize yourself with the language spoken by your interviewers. Even if you are making a lateral move within the same industry, you should know that no two jobs are alike, nor are any two corporations. Before walking into the premises of your prospective employer, try and learn as much as possible about the company and the role you are interviewing for. Managers will recognize that you've done your homework, making you a more desirable candidate. In addition to demonstrating a keen interest in the job, being well prepared also makes it easier to handle questions during an interview.

Before the interview, I try to prepare a client for standard interview questions (Why do you want to leave your current job? Why this company? Why should we hire you?) as well as role-specific questions. In the financial industry, the sell side (investment banks and broker-dealers) and the buy side (money managers and hedge funds) have their own terminology and jargon. A trader at an investment bank is likely to speak of maximizing the "bid-offer spread[9]" whereas a hedge fund manager will be more concerned with "Sharpe Ratio[10]" and "drawdown limits[11]."

Speaking your interviewer's language becomes even more important when you are trying to switch roles within the same industry or migrate across fields. The goal is not to appear to be an expert in the field, but to be able to display a basic grasp of the subject. Sometimes, even comprehending a question requires a working knowledge of the jargon used by your interviewer. A question like "Is your strategy discretionary[12] or black-box[13]?" would be incomprehensible to someone who didn't know the difference between the two terms.

PRACTICE ROLE-PLAY

I have often found role-playing exercises useful to prepare candidates for an upcoming interview. Depending on the situation, I play the role of a candidate or of the interviewer. A simulated interview boosts the individual's confidence while also exposing chinks in their armor.

In the weeks leading up to his job offer, John (from Chapter 3) was nervous about being questioned on the fine points of his deferred compensation buyout. So, he asked me to play him

---

[9] The difference between the buying and the selling price of any security
[10] Most widely used measure of risk versus reward
[11] Maximum allowable loss
[12] Where investment decisions are made by the portfolio manager
[13] Another word for algorithmic trading, where a software program makes buy/sell decisions

while he role-played the company's HR representative.

"How can you prove that your numbers are correct?" he asked. This was the question he was most afraid of because there was no easy way to prove it.

"That's beside the point. It's not like you are buying me out anywhere close to fair value. Even if my valuation is off by a factor of two, three, or even four, you are still getting me at a discount," I replied, offering a potential deflection to an important question.

His next question made me laugh.

"Are you working with Kamal?" he asked, afraid that a previous client of mine, who played an instrumental role in his recruitment, would recognize my negotiating style.

"Kamal who?" I said, without skipping a beat, which made him laugh.

Incidentally, the first question did come up in the conversation, but the second, thankfully, did not.

In another instance, I had to put in a great deal of effort in preparing a researcher for an interview at a hedge fund. Having spent his entire career ensconced in an ivory tower, the poor guy had no idea about how the real world worked. I schooled him in the language that he was likely to encounter during the interview and provided him with answers to the most basic questions. He managed to get through the interviews largely unscathed, and soon enough, the only thing standing between him and a job offer was a reference check.

In an amusing turn of events, he decided to use me as a reference. I would have preferred not to play this role, but he had no other options. The next day, his future boss questioned me about the individual whom I had spent weeks counseling. Needless to say, the job was his.

ISSUES SPECIFIC TO FRESH GRADUATES

Although college students make up only a small fraction of my clientele, I take special care in advising them. Anyone looking for their first job (or internship) faces a challenging time in interviews, as the corporate world can seem especially intimidating. In addition to teaching them how to converse in a corporate setting, I also make sure that every fresh graduate realizes that the company needs them as much, if not more. This simple fact provides a boost to their confidence, thereby making them a better candidate.

When it comes to college students, I pay especially close attention to their résumé. That one-page document serves as your marketing tool, so be extremely careful about what you put on it. Corporations don't expect you to know much at this stage of your life, but they do expect you to be able to defend anything that's on your résumé. So, don't write that you are fluent in Spanish if you aren't—the company will find someone to test you on that point. Likewise, during the years I worked at Lehman Brothers, any candidate whose résumé so much as mentioned gambling would be brought around to my desk for questioning. A thumbs down from me would remove the individual from consideration. If the company believes that you've exaggerated—or worse, fabricated—a part of your background, they are likely to question the rest as well. It is for this reason that I grill college seniors on every aspect of their résumé. If they cannot adequately explain some aspects, I ask them to modify or remove those parts.

While most fresh graduates are likely to face fairly generic questions during their interviews, some companies have specific expectations. Management consulting firms, for instance, expect a candidate to answer their questions in a manner consistent with how these companies communicate with their clients. The only logical conclusion is that they expect these 22-year-olds to immediately start generating revenue instead of investing time and money in training them, as most corporations do with fresh graduates.

In another case, an industrial automation company had a rather unusual requirement for a college senior looking for an entry-level position in sales. They wanted to test the student's negotiating ability.

"How can a company expect a 21-year-old to negotiate the price of its products?" I was incredulous.

"I'm serious," the young man said. "Look at their interview guidelines."

The instructions were crystal clear. Every candidate was expected to participate in a mock negotiation with a potential customer over the price of the company's widgets. So, I gave him a crash course in negotiating, emphasizing that he should try to maximize the total dollar value of the sale rather than the price of individual items. The final result of his negotiation, unfortunately, was disappointing.

"I didn't make the sale," he said as I debriefed him.

"Why?"

"The customer's price was too low."

Once he recounted how the negotiation had unfolded, I was proud of my student. He had offered a 20 percent discount on the product, but the buyer refused to budge from 65 cents on the dollar. My client made every effort to negotiate a higher price before politely walking away.

"I don't care if they don't hire you," I said. " "I would've done the same in your shoes."

The company did hire him, rather quickly too. As it turned out, the managers were more interested in seeing whether the candidate had the spine to turn a client down than in the sale itself. Unbeknownst to us, he had passed the test with flying colors.

HANDLING INAPPROPRIATE QUESTIONS

Speaking the interviewer's language does not mean that you have to answer every question they pose. Sometimes, when managers ask questions they have no business asking, a polite refusal is the best option.

The inappropriate questions frequently, though not always, have to do with an individual's past compensation. This practice was rampant before 2020, when New York state passed a law prohibiting an employer from seeking any information about an applicant's past salary. The law notwithstanding, I have known of unscrupulous managers to say, "I am not supposed to ask this, but what are you getting paid currently?" Before 2020, I knew of several cases of HR trying to bully candidates into revealing their compensation and acting genuinely surprised when my clients refused.

"You are the only candidate who has a problem with this question," was a common reply, thus proving that HR is not above lying either.

At other times, the inappropriate questions have nothing to do with the individual's compensation. During one of my interviews, I was asked for my opinion of a certain individual in the industry. I felt the question was deeply unfair, but I answered it anyway. My answer, "I'm not a fan," did not hurt my employment prospects, but the question remained inappropriate regardless.

In another instance, an interviewer took the same question a bit too far.

"We have both encountered many of the same people in the past. I am going to list a few names, and I want you to tell me what you think of them."

"He had no right to ask you that. I hope you told him to get lost," I said to my client.

"Sadly, no. The question made me deeply uncomfortable, but I answered it anyway."

As it turned out, refusing to answer wouldn't have cost him anything. Despite accommodating his interviewer, his candidacy went no further.

The outcome was the same in another case, where a future manager demanded to know not only if the candidate had received another job offer but also who it was from.

"I'm sorry, but I cannot reveal that information," the individual replied, which is the only right answer to that question.

The manager, however, refused to take no for an answer.

"I need to know if your offer is from one of these companies," he continued, listing the names of their four biggest competitors.

This was truly a ridiculous request. Imagine if the roles were reversed, and an individual demanded that their interviewer reveal the names of other candidates being considered for the position. Undoubtedly, that would mark the end of the interview.

"Again, I'm sorry, but I cannot say anything about the name of the other company," the candidate replied politely but firmly.

"If you won't answer the question, then we won't give you an offer," the annoyed interviewer retorted. Notice the careful wording of the ultimatum. It doesn't say that answering the question will get the candidate hired, only that not answering will not.

The manager was true to his word, and my client never received a job offer. However, I doubt that it was because of his refusal to submit to the manager's demands. If the company had been serious about hiring him, they would not have treated him so callously. My guess is that the manager was gathering intelligence about the competition and had no real interest in the individual.

It is highly inappropriate for any interviewer to go on a fishing expedition that has nothing to do with the job requirements. At the same time, I understand it can be difficult for an individual to stand up to questions from someone who has the power over their getting hired. Still, if a question feels improper, you are much better off replying, "I don't understand how this relates to my ability to perform the job," rather than attempting to fumble through an answer. You might even get points for showing a backbone, as was the case with the college senior above.

IN CONCLUSION

Given that a corporation has to decide about a candidate in a short time, it is imperative for the candidate to make a good first impression. No matter how apprehensive you feel inside, make sure that you are a picture of confidence on the outside. Before any interview, do your homework and learn as much as you can about the company and the position. If needed, practice answering questions by asking a friend to act as an interviewer. And if you encounter uncomfortable questions during an interview, don't be afraid to push back. That may even be what the company wants from a candidate.

CHAPTER 14

TIME YOUR MOVES TO HIDE YOUR POSITION

IN ANY GAME of incomplete information, a player must consider what move to make next and when to make it. Whether it is made swiftly or with careful deliberation, the timing of a move contains additional clues about the strength (or weakness) of a player's position.

Take a poker all-in, for instance. The last thing that a player who puts all of their chips in play wants to see is an instantaneous call. They might as well get up from the table because, in all probability, they've lost the hand. The longer the opponent ponders the question—to call or not to call—the greater the chance that the original bettor wins. Incidentally, a snap call of this nature is usually reserved for those poker hands where one side has made their final move[14]. In virtually every other situation, a poker player thinks carefully about how to time their

---

[14] The very definition of an all-in

moves. Whether they choose to make every bet like clockwork or mix them up randomly, the goal is to not give off a tell. Sometimes, they may react slowly when they have a strong hand, and at other times, do the exact opposite—anything to keep the other side guessing.

The same is true for a negotiation. A negotiator times their responses carefully to conceal the true nature of their position. The negotiator knows that the same reply conveys a different message depending on when (and how) it is delivered. Even the most unsophisticated counterparty will realize that they've made a mistake if their proposal is met with an immediate and enthusiastic, "I'll take it!" If the same reply is delivered the following day, and with a sigh, they are far less likely to believe the same. Moreover, the impact of a response also varies with its timing. A carefully pondered reply is likely to be taken much more seriously than a knee-jerk reaction. Consequently, in any negotiation, it is important to not only formulate the correct response but also to deliver it at the right time.

However, not every situation requires a careful and deliberate response. There are times when an immediate reply carries the greatest punch. The key is knowing when to reply quickly and when to take your time.

WHEN TO TAKE YOUR TIME

I would argue that the majority of job-related negotiations require you to take some time before making your move. Even if the optimal move is apparent to me within minutes of receiving a proposal, I will still wait for hours (or even days) before making it. Remember, the key to a successful outcome is keeping your opponent off-balance, and a quick reply does the exact opposite. No matter what your response, it removes all doubt from your opponent's mind as to where you stand. In contrast, having to wait for hours, if not days, is liable to make them increasingly more nervous about your next move. That is why companies—even those that often take weeks or months to make a decision—expect an immediate reply from their chosen candidate, sometimes while the candidate is still on their premises.

In one of the more extreme examples of this phenomenon, a company once took six whole months before finally making my client an offer. Tucked away in that offer was a short but infuriating line:

"This offer expires on September 25."

The offer had been made on September 22, so the company had given my client all of three days to accept. He ignored the deadline, which prompted a call from his future boss, giving him more time. The boss didn't realize it, but by taking so long to decide, the company had weakened its position. First, the longer the job search, the more vested the company becomes in their final pick, which automatically strengthens the individual's hand. That is why I advise every client to remain compliant, no matter how long a company takes in picking a winner, and then do the exact opposite afterwards. The key to achieving an excellent deal for my client in Chapter 8 was that the position had gone unfilled for almost three months.

Second, and far more important, the long time taken by the company allowed my client to explore other opportunities, one of which he eventually accepted. Had the company gotten its act together and made a final decision in three months instead of six, they would not have lost their chosen candidate.

Another reason to take your time with a response is to not appear overeager. It stands to reason that the company is paying as much attention to the timing of your reply as you are paying to theirs. A quick turnaround on your part (to their offer) is bound to make them believe that you must really want the job. This, in turn, weakens your hand. Likewise, the quicker the company's response to your counterproposal, the stronger your negotiating position.

BUYING TIME

A job offer puts the corporation and the individual on two different timelines. The company wants a quick answer (preferably "yes"), whereas the individual needs to slow the process down and buy time. Therefore, regardless of whether the offer is delivered over the phone or in person, I ask every client to deliver a short speech and quickly get out of dodge:

"Thank you very much for the offer. I want to give it the respect it deserves by thinking carefully about it. I will have a response for you shortly."

No manager dares to refuse this reasonable request. If pressed further, I ask a client to promise a response within 24 hours— long enough for us to determine the next move and short enough to not cause alarm for the company.

While this speech usually does the trick when an offer is first made, it may not work for every back-and-forth conversation with the company. My clients have often needed to employ creative methods to gain time, such as retrieving a nonexistent bag from the airport carousel. Individuals have even taken cover in a restroom to call me for advice while the meeting is in progress. My presence on Andrew's phone call was partly responsible for us gaining the two-and-a-half days that changed everything.

You might need time to respond for several reasons. In addition to evaluating the pros and cons of the offer, you might wish to explore other possibilities. A quick response denies you the ability to do that. You may also want to consider the implications of the company immediately accepting your counterproposal. This issue becomes even more important when pitting companies against each other. As was the case with Andrew, the first company must not know that you are using their offer to get a better one elsewhere. Conversely, the second company must be made aware that time is of the essence. It is astonishing how quickly the wheels of a corporation can turn when there is a risk of losing a candidate to another company. My quick offer from Lehman Brothers was partly the result of the company mistakenly believing that one of their competitors was about to hire me.

I consider a company's demanding a quick response or giving the individual just a handful of days to accept an offer to be bullying tactics. So, they must be resisted by any means necessary.

WHEN TO GIVE A QUICK REPLY

While most job-related negotiations require that you take your time to respond, in some circumstances, a quick reaction is not only justified, but it is also the best move possible. It would be impossible to anticipate all of the scenarios that might require swift action, but two in particular bear mentioning. One of those situations typically occurs at the beginning of the negotiation, and the other, near the end.

There is no point in wasting anyone's time if, in your opinion, the opening offer is not serious. An offer lower than what you are getting paid currently is in this category, requiring a quick, sharp response, as was the case with the researcher and the cancer specialist from Chapter 2. It was impossible for us to know whether the Long Island hospital chain or the West Coast money manager was pulling a fast one, or they simply lacked the ability to pay. No matter what their reasons, both of these situations called for a quick, firm refusal. Taking an entire day to respond to a non-serious offer would have allowed the companies to believe that their offer was legitimate, else you would not need to think about it for so long. Even if the companies believed that they were making a serious offer, a swift negative response would force them to reconsider. Both of those deals fell through, but the money manager did improve their offer by $50,000, no doubt as a result of my client's instant refusal.

Although a high-risk strategy, sometimes an immediate "That's too low" or "We are too far apart" can be an appropriate response to a good offer as well. However, before you attempt a bluff of this sort, make sure that your hand is strong, as the company is likely to react negatively and pull the offer.

Likewise, there is no point in delaying proceedings when negotiations are at an advanced stage and a deal is imminent. Striking while the iron is hot, however, does not imply that you can't ask the company to improve one last time:

"I will accept right now if you would only …"

You will be surprised how often this line produces an even better offer. The key is to ask for something that is within the manager's discretion and not make a demand that requires him to consult with others. Time, at this stage, is more likely to hurt the deal than to help it. So, be prepared to say yes even if your request is denied.

You will recall that in Chapter 12, Andrew fielded five separate offers in the course of just one evening, the result of our near-instantaneous rejection of the company's first four proposals. The merger was only a handful of days away, and it would have been foolish for us to take time over each reply. Instead, by providing quick responses, we made it possible for the company to make a fresh proposal every hour, thereby allowing us to reach a deal by nightfall.

USING TIME EFFECTIVELY

Effectively using time often holds the key to a favorable outcome, as illustrated by one of my negotiations with a hedge fund. I began the negotiation with a swift "no," then refused to respond for an entire week before finally reaching an agreement within minutes.

At the end of a long day of interviews at their offices, the hedge fund's CEO promised that they would let me know of their decision soon. The call came two days later, where he offered me a portfolio manager's job with a percentage payout in the mid-teens. I stopped him mid-sentence.

"That won't work."

"In that case, what do you want?" he asked, as expected.

"Not this," I replied, being difficult on purpose.

The CEO probed me for several minutes, looking for an opening, but I made sure that he got nowhere.

"It's Friday today. Can you let us know on Monday what you would like?"

"Sure," I replied, even though I had no intention of doing so.

I had made it clear while interviewing that in addition to a percentage of my profits, I also expected to be paid a fixed fee, akin to what the hedge fund collected from its investors[15]. Despite that, at no point during our phone call did the CEO bring up that possibility. Moreover, I was convinced that it wasn't an oversight on his part. The company was simply unwilling to share its management fee. If this negotiation was to proceed any further, they would have to yield on that point. So, I didn't call the CEO back for an entire week, the equivalent of a lifetime in these matters.

The following Friday, I heard from the firm's co-CEO.

"You didn't call us."

"We were too far apart," I replied. "There was no point."

"Fine, we will pay you a management fee," he said.

Once the company had crossed that hurdle, the only remaining question was how much. He gave me a number, which I countered, and we agreed to meet halfway. The entire call lasted less than five minutes. The iron was hot, and I didn't waste any time striking it.

---

[15] Hedge funds typically collect a 2 percent management fee and a 20 percent performance fee.

GO WITH THE FLOW

A negotiation can often feel like you are floating down a river. Sometimes, it meanders slowly, apparently going nowhere, and at other times, it plunges you into a whitewater rapid, leaving you out of breath. No matter what stage of the negotiation you are in, it is important to go with the flow and not fight it.

The initial phase of any job search tends to move slowly as the company goes through each candidate. At this stage, you are one of many and have little to no leverage. Consequently, your best move is to wait until the company has winnowed the field of applicants down to a few, if not just one. Whenever that occurs, you will find the process speeding up and managers communicating with you more frequently. Corporations play a lot of games with individuals, but not when it comes to the timing of their moves. In my experience, managers let the chosen candidate know of their decision as soon as it is made. The same holds true at every stage of the negotiation, where bosses typically deliver the company's reply as soon as they are able to.

I can't know for sure, but I suspect this is because a hiring manager is rarely in control of the negotiation. They must seek approval from their bosses or from HR before responding to your counterproposal. This is why I pay close attention to the timing of a company's moves. Their reaction time essentially reflects how long it took them to reach a decision. Whether the response comes within hours or not for days sends a very different signal, and I adjust accordingly. The quicker their response, the faster I react. And if it takes ages to get a response out of the company, I think carefully whether another counterproposal is worth it. Perhaps it is time to just accept the offer.

There are times when a negotiation stalls for no apparent reason, which is an especially frustrating experience. Nevertheless, you should leave it alone and not follow up with the company. The manager knows that they owe you a response, so there must be a good reason for the continued silence, albeit one that they are not willing to share for fear of looking ineffective. That's what happened to a client of mine, where a future manager practically offered him the job over drinks and even discussed compensation. However, for weeks and months after that, the boss ghosted my client. The situation left my client deeply confused. He made numerous attempts to seek clarification, but was unable to get even a single text or email in response. To this date, we have no clue about what happened other than perhaps the manager spoke out of turn and was too embarrassed to admit it.

IN CONCLUSION

When negotiating with a corporation, pay careful attention to the timing of your and your opponent's response. The same words convey a different message depending on when they are delivered. While most situations require that you take your time to respond, there are some that warrant a quick reply. Those usually occur at the beginning of the process or near the end. No matter what the stage of a negotiation, make sure that you go with the flow instead of fighting it.

CHAPTER 15

WIPE THE SLATE CLEAN

THE FIRST THING to do at the end of a successful negotiation is to wipe the slate clean. Once the contract is signed, it is best to forget about the machinations that brought you to this point and concentrate on the task at hand. The moves you made, the stories you spun, and the bluffs you called are history and will have no bearing on your future at the company. If you are wondering whether the corporation will do the same too, the answer is yes. In all my years of negotiating, I have found that the acrimony of even the most fiercely contested negotiation becomes a thing of the past once a deal has been consummated. I do not know of a single instance when an individual, once hired, suffered any consequences for playing hard to get. If anything, managers have frequently complimented them for being good negotiators. If more people were aware of this fact, they would be less bashful in negotiating with a future employer.

I learned this lesson at an early age by watching my mother bargain with shopkeepers in New Delhi. Whenever she walked into a store, it was as if the past did not exist. The same merchants who had complained that she was taking food from their children's mouths the day before showed no hesitation in bargaining with her all over again. They were clearly still making a profit, albeit a little less than from other customers. Her antics made me realize that the key to a business relationship was to wipe the slate clean after every encounter, a principle that I have consistently adhered to. I know that the corporation is still making a profit from my or my client's work, albeit a little less than from other employees. Therefore, no matter how much a manager protests during a negotiation, I am confident that there will be no hard feelings afterwards.

Putting the negotiation behind you doesn't mean that you forget the lessons learned; those should stay with you always and prove useful in your next negotiation. Nevertheless, you must now consider how to manage your new employer.

A JOB IS A BUSINESS RELATIONSHIP

There is no other way to think of a job other than a business relationship with your employer. You provide a service, and the company compensates you for it. The only difference between you and a supplier is that you are selling your time, and not physical goods. Any business relationship needs to be constantly reevaluated, rationally and without emotion. You may like your coworkers, but that is not the primary reason for your being at the company, nor is it theirs. Similarly, any idea of loyalty to the corporation should be disregarded because it is one-sided. No corporation has ever hesitated to get rid of employees if it furthers their objectives. Any CEO who talks of loyalty to employees is lying. If there is anything that corporations are loyal to, it is higher profits.

Navigating this treacherous landscape is challenging, and it requires you to carry as little baggage as possible. Hence, I constantly advise clients to focus on the here and now, not on their past experiences. The past, whether good or bad, will only hold you back. Andrew's unpleasant experience with one broker-dealer nearly caused him to turn down a great offer from another. With the benefit of 15 years of hindsight, there is no doubt that he made the correct choice, even though he had to be pushed into making it.

Similarly, I have known of individuals who signed terrible contracts because they "trusted" their future bosses, only to be rudely awakened down the line. This is another example of an individual allowing past interactions to cloud their thinking about the future. They would have been much better off examining the situation dispassionately, with a fresh pair of eyes.

WHAT HAVE YOU DONE FOR ME LATELY?

You should avoid getting too comfortable in a job because while it is here today, it could be gone tomorrow. That does not mean that you cannot have a long-term relationship with your employer. You can, but only by staying watchful and watching out for your own interests. If at any point you find your goals diverging from the company's, I would cut bait, no matter how painful it is. You cannot stay in a bad situation simply because it was good in the past. For five years, I was thrilled to be working at a Swiss bank; yet, I decided to leave the moment I realized it was a house of cards. No personal relationships were worth sacrificing my reputation or my future for.

I recommend that you too view any employer with a healthy dose of skepticism. Even if you are happy at work today, there is no guarantee that the situation will persist. The corporate landscape is ever changing, and companies routinely transform themselves unrecognizably. Boeing's recent troubles can be traced back to its 1997 merger with McDonnell Douglas, which led to a dramatic change in the storied company's culture and strategy. That shift in focus from quality to profits has a lot to do with the company's reputation being in tatters today.

It is often difficult for an individual to understand, or even be aware of, all the changes taking place at high levels of the organization. Still, those decisions will eventually filter down and provide you with a clue. In my case, it was a passing comment from my boss, "You have the highest hit ratio of anyone here; yet, everyone else makes more money than you." That statement opened my eyes to the real situation at the Swiss bank and led to my departure. With Boeing, I would argue that the truth was hiding in plain sight. From 1998 to 2018, the company spent an astonishing $61 billion on stock buybacks, money that would have been better spent on research and development. The irony is, buybacks or no buybacks, the company has lost a staggering $200 billion in market value from its 2019 peak[16], the result of its many well-publicized scandals.

The moral of the story is that you should never give your employer the benefit of doubt because, whether you realize it

---

[16] As of March 2025

or not, they aren't giving you the benefit of doubt either. No matter what your bosses say, you will find yourself on the street if you cease to be useful. Hence, you should view corporate America through the same lens it uses to view you: What have you done for me lately?

NEGOTIATING WITH YOUR CURRENT EMPLOYER

At its core, the relationship between an employee and an employer is transactional. As with any such relationship, it requires periodic adjustment to the terms of the deal. Consequently, there will be times when you have to negotiate with your current employer, but that process is quite different from negotiating with a future employer. With the latter, you can afford to be ruthless, but dealing with the former requires finesse.

When attempting to negotiate with your current employer, you can ignore how you got here in the first place. The concessions that your bosses made to bring you on board are akin to the special discounts businesses offer to new customers. Now that you are an established customer, the same discounts are no longer valid, and new rules apply instead.

The mere act of asking for something, be it more money or greater responsibility, reveals your dissatisfaction with the current state of affairs. Given that corporations are relentlessly focused on what you've done for them lately, it makes sense to expose yourself only when your performance hits a short-term peak. Every job has its own ebb and flow, and a slump is usually not the best time to make demands.

The operative word while dealing with a current employer

is "gently." An aggressive stance will only antagonize your boss, which is the last thing you need. Instead, your goal should be to recruit your boss as an ally so they can advocate your case to the powers that be. Logical and well-reasoned arguments go a long way toward bringing a manager to your side. As discussed earlier, you should never use another employee's pay as a reason for why you should get paid more. Instead, it is best to stick to issues such as your position's market value and your job performance when arguing for an increase in compensation. You should also never give your bosses an ultimatum or threaten to quit if you don't get your way. Every job in the United States is presumed to be "at will," which means that either side can terminate the relationship whenever they like. Every boss knows this basic fact, and there's nothing to be gained by stating it explicitly. Incidentally, this is the opposite of the approach to take with a company that's trying to hire you. There, you should feel free to say, "If you don't give me what I want, then I'm not coming."

I have come across managers who have told my clients, "If you want to get paid more, then go get another offer." I find this approach to be, for the lack of better words, dumb and short-sighted. First, it demonstrates that the bosses lack the confidence to determine the individual's pay themselves. Instead, they seek validation from another entity, most likely a competitor. Second and more important, once an employee goes to the trouble of getting a competing offer, there is every chance that they will take it. A manager's goal should be to keep an employee satisfied enough so they don't go looking elsewhere, not shove them into the arms of another company.

WHEN YOU ARE BETTER OFF STAYING

Sometimes, though, the act of looking outside the company can make the individual realize that they are better off staying in their present employment, something that has happened to me on multiple occasions. I once walked out of a Morgan Stanley interview because a manager tried to bully me into disclosing my investment methodology. Similarly, I have turned several hedge funds down for various reasons and continued working at the same job.

The decision to stay does not imply that you have lost the ability to negotiate with your employer. It requires some finesse, but you can still ask for more money by offering the company something in return.

This was the situation in which Jane, a marketing manager at a West Coast radio station chain, found herself. A music streaming service had expressed interest in hiring her for a similar role. She was excited at the prospect of leaving old media for new and the potential increase in salary. However, after an afternoon of interviews at the company's headquarters, she realized that she didn't belong there. She decided to stay on at her current job, but she still wanted that pay increase. The situation was especially tricky because the company had only recently increased her salary from $100,000 a year to $120,000.

"What are you looking for?" I asked.

"$150,000," she replied, without any hesitation.

Jane had done her homework. She had attended several industry conferences and even spoken at a few, where she learned the going rate for her position. But she felt uncomfortable marching into her boss's office and asking for another raise so soon after the previous one.

"I think you will have to give the company something in return for a higher salary," I said.

"What can I offer them?"

"Are you okay with not getting another raise for three years if they increase your pay to $150,000?"

"Absolutely!"

"In that case, let your boss know that while you are very happy with your job, your compensation is not quite at market rate. You would like your salary to go up to $150,000, and in return, you will sign a three-year contract. This way, the company can count on your commitment for the next three years and also on your not asking for another raise during that period."

"Understood."

I didn't hear from Jane for a few days, which meant that things were proceeding according to plan. Subsequently, I received a two-word email from her, "Mission accomplished."

When the contracts had been signed, Jane said something that has stayed with me to this day.

"You don't know what this means to me, Kamal. This $30,000 a year will pay for my kids' college tuition."

The simple statement made this one of the most satisfying negotiations I have been involved in.

DEALING WITH CONFLICT AT WORK

No matter how hard you try to avoid it, conflict is inevitable in any job, more so in large corporations. By definition, the larger the company, the more bureaucratic its structure and the more complicated its organizational chart. It is, therefore, not difficult to imagine situations where someone might step on your toes. Although sometimes inadvertent, more often than not, such actions tend to be turf grabs by the other party. The more insecure an individual feels about their position within the company, the greater the probability that they will pull a move of this nature. Alternatively, they may be overly ambitious and see an advantage in laying claim to your domain. Regardless of motivations, any such act of aggression must be dealt with, if for no other reason than to preserve your self-respect. There is also the possibility that if you give an inch today, they will take a mile tomorrow.

There are several parallels between negotiating and dealing with work-related conflict. At its heart, every negotiation is a conflict where the two sides have diametrically opposite objectives. It stands to reason, therefore, that many of the same rules apply to both.

I advise clients to engage in conflict only as a matter of defense, never offensively. I do not shy away from conflict, but I rarely initiate it. In addition, I believe in sticking to a few principles while engaging in a battle at work: Don't display anger, never make it personal, and always focus on the future.

A show of emotion is almost never a good idea at work. No matter how you feel inside, it is vital to be calm on the outside as you try and resolve the situation. Much like when negotiating with your employer, you need to recruit your manager as an ally by making a rational case for your position. If your manager is the source of your problems, then I would advise you to not put up a fight and simply leave the company. In my experience, corporations are loath to side with an underling over a manager because doing so would call into question the judgment of its higher-ups. After all, it is senior management who appointed this manager in the first place. As mentioned before, corporations will go to great lengths to protect themselves and their own. They would rather sacrifice a valuable employee than create doubt about their own judgment.

Even in situations that have gone too far, a show of anger is unwarranted. You should have rightfully spoken up before things escalated. So, don't compound the first error by making another one and acting irrationally. I knew the situation at the Swiss bank was beyond repair, so I left quietly, without saying a word to anyone.

A workplace conflict can never be made personal. No matter how strongly you feel about the other party, they cannot be the central theme of your argument. Instead, maintain your focus on what's in the company's best interests, and if possible, also your boss's. Only then is there any hope of resolving the conflict in your favor. If you find yourself unable to make such an argument, then it's best to not pick a fight.

Finally, try not to bring up the past in any conflict and focus on the future instead. An airing of past grievances will give rise to the obvious question, "Why didn't you say anything then?" If you must bring up the history of the matter, it should only be to provide context, not with the intent of righting past wrongs. To the extent possible, avoid using the words "should have" while arguing for your point of view.

Despite your best efforts, there will be times when you'll lose the fight. Whenever that occurs, accept defeat gracefully and start looking for another job.

IN CONCLUSION

The end of an employment-related negotiation invariably marks the start of a new job and requires you to turn your attention toward managing your relationship with the company. Be aware that the relationship is purely transactional, and don't get too comfortable in any job. The corporation you join may look very different in the years that follow. Stay watchful for those changes and leave if your goals diverge from the company's. Don't hesitate to ask for a periodic adjustment to your terms of employment, but do so gently. And if you find yourself in a conflict at work, make sure you tackle it in a cool, calm, and collected manner.

CHAPTER 16

THERE IS NO SILVER BULLET

THERE IS NO silver bullet for a successful negotiation. No single rule or tactic will cause your opponent to magically capitulate and give in to your demands. A successful outcome requires you to focus on the process and make good decisions at every step. As long as every move is made carefully and correctly, the final result usually takes care of itself.

The rules presented in this book are overarching principles, rather than recipes for handling specific situations. I have included real-life examples to illustrate my points, but I don't expect any of those to mirror your particular circumstances. Over the past 25 years, I cannot recall any two negotiations that were even similar, let alone identical. Each encounter had its own nuances and idiosyncrasies, which is why the first rule in this book focuses on adaptability above all else. In all likelihood, any negotiation will require a combination of the rules listed herein and possibly a few more that you may have to invent yourself. However, I would urge you to not sacrifice your principles in an attempt to be adaptable. Some things in life are not negotiable.

For instance, I have no qualms about misleading an opponent, but I have never allowed a client to lie in order to accomplish that goal. Likewise, I have never accepted payment for my services, no matter how high the amounts involved. Nor have I deviated from my primary objective of securing the best possible deal for every client. I may not have always succeeded, but there has never been any doubt about where my loyalties lie.

RECOGNIZE A NON-NEGOTIABLE SITUATION

The first thing a negotiator must do is to ascertain whether the circumstances even warrant a negotiation—because not every situation does. That was the case with my shortest-duration client—a duration of just one phone call. She had been fired by her employer, and several high-priced lawyers had advised her to put up a fight[17]. Deep down, though, she knew that the company had fired her because they didn't need her anymore, not because she was a woman. Moreover, despite the fact that they were not legally required to do so, the company had offered a generous severance package totaling several hundred thousand dollars. As I went through her employment and separation agreements, I was left with one burning question.

"What exactly do you hope to achieve by fighting?"

"I am not sure."

"If you are not sure, then don't fight. Take the money and run."

That was the end of our discussion, and she signed the

---

[17] They had also asked for a $30,000 retainer.

papers the next day. Incidentally, this situation not only did not require negotiating, but it was also non-negotiable. The company knew full well that they had made an excellent offer, and as if to prove it, they had signed the separation agreement before sending it to her. While this is not a rule, I have found that a signed contract is less open to modification than one that is considered to be a draft. That was also the case when a manager flew cross-country to make an offer to my client. How can you ask for more money from someone who travels 3,000 miles to present a job offer in person?

Similarly, in 2018, I purposefully chose not to negotiate with a hedge fund startup. The founder had hired me at Lehman Brothers 25 years earlier and given me a shot at a career in high finance. So, I figured it was my turn to return the favor. Even though I had considerable leverage in the situation—the company had hardly any employees—it felt unseemly to make demands. That turned out to be a good move. A few months later, that small startup became the largest hedge fund launch in history and provided me with the perfect ending to my memoir.

NO VICTORY LAP

The last thing anyone should do at the end of a successful negotiation is to gloat. Even if you've won a great victory, you must pretend that you've lost. There is little point in showing up an opponent who will soon be your boss. Even in negotiations that do not involve a job offer, it must appear as if you are the one conceding. The final offer, therefore, is always grudgingly accepted.

At the end of one of my negotiations, the company wanted to insert a clause that would allow them to terminate the contract for a fee. Even though I had an amount in mind for the fee, I asked them for a number.

"We'll get back to you."

When it came, their proposal made my jaw drop. They were offering twice what I would have accepted. So, I waited a couple of hours and called them back.

"I think this matter has gone on for long enough. That's fine. I'll just accept your terms," I said, with a sense of abject resignation.

However, it is not enough to be glum on the outside as you celebrate on the inside—you must also keep the victory to yourself and maybe a few trusted friends. The world is a small place, and there is every chance that word of your bragging will reach your bosses. While managers will forgive the tactics you employed during the negotiation, they will remember this humiliation and make you pay for it.

A signed contract denotes the conclusion of one game, but it frequently marks the beginning of another. The two sides have entered into a business relationship, whether of an employer–employee or buyer–seller. Alerting your opponent to their mistake only serves to hurt your future dealings with them. Even if they are thrilled with the outcome—yes, it is possible for both sides to feel victorious—word of your celebration will invariably lead to worse terms the next time around. Given that business dealings are rarely one and done, it is vital to think about the long run.

THE SCOURGE OF THE NON-COMPETE

No other phenomenon illustrates the predatory nature of employers more than the proliferation of the non-compete clause. A long-standing fixture in senior employees' contracts, these clauses have now found their way into the most pedestrian of jobs, such as those of fast-food workers. The sole purpose of forcing an ex-employee to sit at home for months or years, often without pay, is to reduce their market value. The lack of a non-compete would lead to a dynamic, vibrant, and mobile workforce, which is the last thing a corporation wants. Hiring a new employee is expensive; so, to the extent possible, every company would like to see its personnel locked in place, unable to move. A non-compete accomplishes that objective by making a mockery of "at-will" employment. You are free to leave whenever you like, but you are not free to earn a living elsewhere. Incidentally, companies are careful not to impose any sort of non-competes on themselves. They can hire your replacement tomorrow even as they force you to languish at home for an indeterminate period of time.

This is what makes non-competes so insidious: You don't know how long it's going to be. In virtually every employment agreement I have ever reviewed, reducing the duration of the non-compete is at the company's sole discretion. Consequently, you have no idea when you will be able to start a new job. It could be within a few weeks or not for a year. That uncertainty, once again, reduces your market value, which suits the employers just fine.

Corporations contend that they require these clauses to protect their trade secrets. However, I would argue that employment contracts already prohibit an employee from revealing any confidential information about an ex-employer's business. Moreover, a non-compete does nothing to prevent an ex-employee from disclosing those secrets if they (unwisely) choose to do so. Just because an ex-employee is sitting at home for a year does not mean that they cannot converse with their future employer. Thus, the only purpose of having a non-compete clause on top of confidentiality and non-solicitation clauses is to lower the going rate for labor.

I have not always succeeded, but I have fought every non-compete that has come my way. In some cases, such as Andrew's, the duration of the non-compete has been the deciding factor for accepting or turning down a job. In other cases, I have been able to charge a company for imposing a longer non-compete—time is money after all. Therefore, I urge you to examine the non-compete clause of your employment contract carefully, and if possible, try to negotiate it downward.

In April 2024, the Federal Trade Commission announced a long-overdue plan to ban non-competes from employment agreements. I sincerely hope that I am wrong about this, but I am not optimistic about the final result. Several corporations have already cried foul and come out fighting against this proposed rule. I have little doubt that even if they are unable to kill the proposed ban, they will succeed in watering it down. The last thing a corporation wants is for the playing field to tilt even slightly back in favor of its employees. Big business loves the status quo, and for that reason alone, change is desperately needed.

HOW TO QUIT A JOB

I find the act of quitting a job to be immensely empowering. A resignation, in effect, declares victory over the corporation by sending a message that you can do better elsewhere.

Nevertheless, quitting presents its own challenges and must be handled with care. It places you in direct conflict with your employer because no company wants an employee to leave voluntarily. Managers prefer terminating workers as and when it suits the corporation's purpose. If you are employed, it is proof that you are of some use to them. Consequently, your resignation will likely require the hiring of a replacement, which is both time-consuming and expensive. If big business had their way, they would have their workers locked in place, unable to switch jobs. This is why employment contracts contain clauses whose sole purpose is to restrict an employee's freedom of movement, such as the aforementioned non-compete.

As with any conflict, quitting too requires a thoughtful and unemotional approach. No matter how great your dissatisfaction with the current state of affairs, you must resist the urge to vent. The last thing you need while leaving a job is to make enemies. Corporations have a long reach, and it is impossible to predict how a poorly executed resignation could impact you negatively in the future. Therefore, it is best to leave gracefully and without saying anything negative about the company or your managers. When asked for the reasons why you are leaving, it is best to emphasize the positive aspects of your move, such as future career prospects or your desire to pursue something different.

Another reason to handle your bosses gently is to leave open the possibility that the company might make you a counteroffer. I caution every client that having a signed contract from a future employer is no guarantee that they will actually end up at the new company. I have been involved in numerous situations where an individual trying to leave a company has instead been turned around by a compelling offer from their employer. In such situations, much like any negotiation with a future employer, I insist that the current employer make the opening offer. Consequently, the question "What can we do to make you stay?" must always be answered evasively:

"I haven't given it much thought. What can you do?"

In multiple instances, the answer to this question has surprised me. When faced with the threat of a valued employee leaving, managers frequently end up conceding too much. This is why (as discussed in Chapter 8) you should never disclose what the other company is paying you, as that will automatically place a ceiling on any counteroffer from your current company. No company wants to pay above the market rate for an employee, so it is best to leave them in the dark about the terms of your offer. If they insist on knowing, simply say that the contract requires you to keep that information confidential. Remember that you are in the driving seat here and your bosses are in no position to make demands. If anything, they must handle you with kid gloves if they hope to convince you to stay.

You should also avoid disclosing the name of your future employer and allow your bosses to assume the worst. There are exceptions to this rule—as observed in the case of Goldman Sachs versus Credit Suisse in Chapter 5—but they are few and far between. Companies will try desperately to find out where an employee is going, but they have no right to that information. So, deflect by saying something along the lines of, "I will let you know when I've made a final decision. All that matters at the moment is that I am resigning from my current position." That statement creates the impression that you might have multiple job offers, which will put your bosses further on the defensive and might lead to a better counteroffer.

A resignation must always be announced to your immediate supervisor and no one else. There is nothing to be gained by informing your colleagues beforehand and forcing them to choose between you and the company (you will lose). You can go back to being friends with them once your departure is finalized. In the meantime, leave them out of the process and focus on your chain of command.

Start by quitting verbally and offer a written resignation so your manager knows that you're not bluffing. I prefer not to start with a formal letter because that arrow cannot be put back in the quiver. An official resignation triggers a chain of events, including the crucial step of informing HR. In my experience, managers prefer to control the narrative, not only with their own bosses and HR but also with your coworkers. So, allow them the courtesy of doing so. If you get hauled in front of senior management, politely listen to their pitch about why you are making a mistake. They are bound to ask the same questions that your manager did—where you are going and what you are getting paid—and you should once again refuse to answer. Your only goal in these conversations is for your bosses to give up and say, "Fine, we will let HR know." At that point, you are home free because HR will simply process your departure, and not try to convince you to stay.

Ideally, you would also want your bosses to say that the door is open and that you can return if you are unhappy in your new role. I have known of several instances where an individual left a company, realized they had made a mistake, and returned to the fold within days or weeks. However, this is not always possible, so don't count on it. You should leave a job only when you are convinced that there is a better future for you elsewhere, even if that means being unemployed for a while.

A FINAL WORD

I consider negotiating to be an act of great optimism. No matter how difficult the situation, a negotiator believes that a better deal is just around the corner. A pessimist, on the other hand, wouldn't even bother trying, as they would have no hope of success.

My optimism persists despite a growing disillusionment with the current landscape. The power of corporations notwithstanding, it is still possible to negotiate with them and secure at least a fair deal. My hope with this book is to inspire readers to enter their next work-related negotiation with a sense of courage and hope. While I harbor no grand illusions about changing the world, I do believe that it would be a less unfair place if everyone learned how to negotiate. I have lost count of the number of times a successful negotiation has positively impacted a client's life. Even in situations where the outcome was less than ideal, there was satisfaction in having tried. It is far better to have fought and lost than to have surrendered meekly. The former preserves your self-respect while the latter leaves you wondering, "What if...?"

The final outcome of a negotiation is not in your control—there are simply too many variables. How you choose to play the game, however, is entirely your choice. It is, therefore, of vital importance that you learn to play this game well. After all, if you won't stand up for yourself, who will?

ACKNOWLEDGEMENTS

First and foremost, I would like to thank my literary agent, Sam Hiyate, who had the vision to reimagine my original 2020 manuscript as two distinct books. The first was my memoir, *Play It Right*, published in 2022, and the second is this book. I am also immensely grateful to Mita Kapur for her outstanding work marketing both books in India.

A heartfelt thank you to Jessica Wan for once again meticulously reviewing every rewrite and offering invaluable suggestions. Many thanks to Sharad Chaudhary for his thoughtful assistance throughout this venture and for conceiving the title, *Negotiate It Right*. In hindsight, this book could have no other name. I am also thankful to my beta readers—Amitabh Gupta, Raj Hathiramani, Aditi Gupta, and Michael Phillips—for providing incredibly helpful feedback. A special thank you to the entire Jaico Publishing House team for their dedicated efforts in bringing this book to life. They have been an absolute joy to work with. Last but not least, I would like to express my deepest gratitude to my wife, Kathleen, for her unwavering love and support over the last three decades, as well as for being my in-house editor.

In closing, I want to thank everyone who entrusted me to be their negotiator. Without them, this book would not have been possible.